"In 1940, at the age of eight, I dreamed that one day I would own the best restaurant in the world. All of the customers would love my food, and all of my employees would do everything they were supposed to do. But most important, everyone would think I was a good boss, and every day when I walked into the restaurant, people would be glad to see me. Today, people seem glad to see me in about four thousand Wendy's restaurants. I never expected it to turn out that way . . ."

"Absorbing . . . Dave writes like he talks. He is a down-to-earth, lovable genius."
—Dr. Norman Vincent Peale

"The reader is left with a good feeling of having walked the road with an honorable man, from humble beginning to the realization of the American dream."
—H. Keith H. Brodie, M.D., President, Duke University

"Wendy's is my favorite place for burgers. Now, Dave Thomas is one of my favorite business gurus."
—Bill Fromm, author of *The Ten Commandments of Business and How to Break Them*

DAVE'S WAY

A New Approach to Old-Fashioned Success

R. DAVID THOMAS
Founder of WENDY'S INTERNATIONAL
with RON BEYMA and MARY MAROON GELPI

B

BERKLEY BOOKS, NEW YORK

Wendy's is a trademark of Wendy's International, Inc.

This Berkley book contains the complete text of the original hardcover edition. It has been completely reset in a typeface designed for easy reading, and was printed from new film.

DAVE'S WAY

A Berkley Book / published by arrangement with the author

PRINTING HISTORY
G.P. Putnam's Sons edition / September 1991
Published simultaneously in Canada
Berkley edition / October 1992

ISBN: 0-425-13501-2

A BERKLEY BOOK® TM 757,375
Berkley Books are published by
The Berkley Publishing Group,
200 Madison Avenue, New York, New York 10016.
The name "BERKLEY" and the "B" logo are trademarks belonging to Berkley Publishing Corporation.

PRINTED IN THE UNITED STATES OF AMERICA

10 9 8 7 6 5 4

This book is dedicated to Lorraine, my loving wife of thirty-seven years; my five children—Pam, Kenny, Molly, Wendy, and Lori—both as individuals and as that unshakable bond called the *Thomas Family*; and to the thousands of children who are waiting for adoption and the love of a permanent family.

The author will donate his profits from this book to the cause of adoption—to help children find loving families.

A Special Message from R. David Thomas . . .

When President Bush asked me to be a national spokesman for the "Adoption Works . . . For Everyone" campaign, he challenged me to encourage people to consider adoption. I took the challenge very personally. You see, I was adopted.

So, when *Dave's Way* was first published in hardcover, I figured one way to show my support was to donate my profits from book sales to the cause of adoption. I'm happy to say that there were profits!

Some of these profits have been used to create the guide to adoption you'll find added to the back of this book. This guide, called "Adoption Works . . . For Everyone," is also being distributed nationwide by adoption groups to offer some basic information to people who are considering adopting a child.

There are a lot of myths and misunderstandings about adoption. For one thing, it's not as simple to adopt as it should be, but the experts tell me those who are pleasantly persistent usually are successful. Hopefully, this guide helps explain what adoption really means, and a little about how it works. The fact is that with adoption comes joy and challenges and, always, blessings.

If you're thinking of starting a family, or adding another member to your present family, please consider adopting a child who has been waiting—sometimes a long time—for someone to love them and provide a happy home.

You'll be giving a precious gift to someone who otherwise might never know the special love of a family.

Dave Thomas

CONTENTS

FOREWORD

Let me say just a couple of words about how this book is written.

In *Dave's Way,* I offer some advice. Not all of it will work for everybody. I'm no psychologist, and I'm no economist or big deal politician, either. My goal is to share with you what my life has taught me rather than pretend to tell you what everybody should think or do.

Know in advance that this book probably won't help your grammar. They may even end up sticking a warning label on it from the Grammar General's Office in Washington saying, "CAUTION: Dave Thomas may be hazardous to your sentence structure." So, if I say "real excited" instead of "really excited," it's because that's the way I talk. (In fact, that's the way most people talk, but we won't get into that.) So, you may want to keep my book out of the hands of sixth-graders who are diagramming sentences, or whatever they are doing to sentences these days. On the other hand, the spelling is perfect.

● ● ●

A book never gets written without help from many individuals, and I have been particularly blessed by the people who brought *Dave's Way* to life.

Charlie Rath took my ten-year dream of writing this book and made it a reality. Charlie's sense of humor is very much like my own. I admire how easily he works with people and his knack for making a point through telling a story. Because he is a born marketer, he naturally understands how to get a message across to the guy on the street. Underneath his low-key exterior is a mind that really understands big-time marketing and how to communicate an idea.

Denny Lynch attacked this project with the same enthusiasm he uses when approaching his work at Wendy's. He has a remarkable gift for organizing a project and making sure all the details fall into place. But he also offers a lot more . . . including asking the right, penetrating questions about the big picture. Most of all, he's a perfectionist, who's not happy until the last "t" is crossed. I like that.

Roger Cooper at the Putnam Berkley Group believed that what I had to say might be useful to others.

Ron Beyma came to my rescue and organized my fragmented thoughts into a readable manuscript. His command of prose was crucial in allowing me to write my thoughts in simple sentences.

Rena Wolner and Chris Pepe, my editors at Putnam, knew exactly how to edit the book so the reader could understand the lessons in my life.

There were many people I relied upon for sound advice and support on this project, including my agent, Reid Boates, and Josh Howell, Nancy Weltchek, and Anthony Ramos at Hill and Knowlton. Bob Dilenschneider, the CEO at Hill and Knowlton, always gave prudent counsel when we needed it. Fran Jabara and Dr. Billy Jones, disciples of free enterprise at Wichita State University, provided the early inspiration for this book. And Mary Gelpi devoted almost a year to research my early years and young business career and help me bring them to life.

There would never be a *Dave's Way* without the helping hands of many people who served as my mentors: Minnie Sinclair, George and Frank Regas, Colonel Harland Sanders, Phil Clauss, and Kenny King. You'll learn more about them in this book.

Others who made major contributions to my life's work (Wendy's) include the late Danny Thomas (no relation), who was one of the first investors to back me, and our early franchise owners, like L. S. Hartsog and Jack Massey, who added credibility to the term "Wendy's Franchisee" when they joined our family. They were part of a group of independent entrepreneurs who became franchise owners and are the backbone of Wendy's. I owe an awful lot to our three hundred franchisees, who have invested a sizable financial stake in our success. I wish I could name every single franchisee, but that's impossible.

No discussion about Wendy's success would be complete without paying an enormous tribute to Bob Barney. He was my partner for twenty-five years, and a good friend. He was right next to me during the anxious moments and the euphoric highs as Wendy's grew from a single restaurant into a worldwide company. I hope his years in retirement are joyous and peaceful.

There are two other groups that have contributed dearly to *Dave's Way:*

Our shareholders have been loyal supporters of the Wendy's concept throughout the years, even during the mid-eighties when we may not have been a very good investment. I appreciate this tremendous support and am committed to providing them with a favorable return throughout the 1990s.

I've saved my favorite people for these last words—the men

and women who work for Wendy's around the world. I use "I" and "me" a lot in this book, but no one should even consider that I am solely responsible for our company's success. My colleagues in the restaurants are the real heroes at Wendy's. Every day they must perform a multitude of functions with one paramount goal in mind: providing each customer with a totally satisfying experience.

I have the utmost respect for these people and those in support positions in our area and corporate offices. I am awed by how much we depend on them.

Finally, I'd like to thank our customers. It is because people love to eat out that an adopted boy with little formal education could grab the American dream with both hands. You are the people that let me build a restaurant chain named after my daughter. And it's dreams like mine, which have been repeated countless times across this land, that have made America the greatest country in the world.

Dave Thomas

September 1991
Fort Lauderdale, FL

PART I

1

Nobody Special

In 1940, at the age of eight, I dreamed that I would one day own the best restaurant in the world. All of the customers would love my food, and all of my employees would do everything they were supposed to do. But, most important, everyone would think I was a good boss, and every day when I walked into the restaurant, people would be glad to see me.

Today, people seem glad to see me in about four thousand Wendy's restaurants. In roughly thirty years, the fast-food business has gone from nothing to a nearly $70-billion-dollar industry. It has turned jobs into careers for many people. And it has given me the biggest single stake in one of America's largest restaurant chains, making me a millionaire many times over. I never expected it to be that way.

When Wendy's began in 1969, I saw the chance to have perhaps three or four restaurants in the Columbus, Ohio, area. When we built those and they worked, the company grew, and still more opportunities opened up. Opportunity never knocked, but it was all around us. You just had to see it, and we were lucky enough to do that.

A few months ago, some Wendy's corporate officers and I

drove up in front of New York's posh Waldorf-Astoria Hotel
in a black stretch limousine. We were headed for a Wendy's
operator meeting, and the limo was rented, but that didn't
stop the curiosity-seekers in front of the hotel. When I got
out, one elderly lady grabbed my arm and said, "I've seen you
somewhere. Are you important?"

"I'm nobody, really," I answered. "I just make hamburgers
for a living." Then she caught sight of my red-and-yellow
Wendy's lapel pin.

"Oh, you must be that Mr. Wendy guy on TV. I like your
ads." Before I could say anything, she smiled smugly and
rushed off.

I know plenty of celebrities—Frank Sinatra and Bob Hope
and lots of others. The biggest celebrity I know is George
Bush, and he asked me to lead a campaign on adoption
awareness, but I myself am no celebrity and never want to be
one. The only autograph I give that gets plenty of hugs and
kisses is on a check to one of my kids. And, I'll add right now,
they are good kids who have done plenty with their lives.

From the very beginning, I never thought of myself as
anybody special. As a child I mostly thought of myself as
alone. Some people can remember back to when they were
three years old. Some can only go back to age ten or eleven.
I can remember back to when I was five. The first memory I
have of my mother (who, I learned later, was my adoptive[1]
mother) is when she was sick. (She died soon after, and at the
time I really didn't understand what death meant.)

Her name was Auleva and she died of rheumatic fever. I
really don't remember her, what she looked like or how she

---

[1]Everybody says foster mother for adoptive mother and I used to, too.
"Adoptive" still sounds a little long and strange to me, but I'm committed
to using it—because it's the right word to use.

treated me. But I *do* remember when she was really sick, and when she died. No one really explained anything, but I remember the smell of her hospital room and how white everything was: her face, the sheets, the floor, the nurses. By contrast, everything was so colorful at the funeral home, and there were flowers and people everywhere. It scared me to be around so many people because I wasn't used to strangers. We never had any visitors come to our house, and I wasn't sure how I was supposed to act. But they were all nice to me, and they all seemed to really like my mother.

The whole thing was like a strange dream to me. I didn't know people were supposed to die, and I didn't know who would replace her. When I saw my mother's casket lowered into the ground at the cemetery it bothered me a lot. My adoptive grandmother, Minnie Sinclair, explained that my mother had gone to heaven where she would watch over me.

When I was a little kid, Minnie Sinclair was the strongest influence in my life. I lived with her during the summer months till I was about eight or nine, and I really liked being around her. She lived in Michigan, but she was born and raised in the hills of Kentucky. I had a lot of respect for her. She had so little, but she made so much out of it. Minnie was a real strong-willed lady. She believed if you worked hard, you made things happen. And, she was a hard worker and she provided. Her two brothers worked in WPA (Works Projects Administration) during the Depression. She was a diehard Republican and really liked Tom Dewey. In fact, when she found out that one of her brothers voted for Franklin Roosevelt, she made him sleep out in the barn.

Minnie raised all four of her children all by herself after her husband was killed working on the railroad. "I took whatever work I could find after Grandpa died," she told me. "Hard work is good for the soul, and it keeps you from feeling sorry for yourself because you don't have time. Four kids were depending on me and I just knew that the Lord would provide, and He did. All my kids grew up to be fine people, David, and your mother was one of the finest. I prayed and prayed and the Almighty heard my prayers."

I remember my grandmother (I didn't know she was my adoptive grandmother until later) praying a lot. She would mumble prayers to herself, and she would pray out loud, too. She was the most religious person I knew. She worshipped God, loved Jesus, and read the Bible every day. "If you want to go to heaven you've got to accept the suffering God sends your way. All good Christians have pain, David," she told me when my mother died. "It's the price we pay for eternal peace and happiness. Your mother had pain and now she is at rest."

I thought my grandmother was pretty. She was of average height and weight, but she had marvelous hands: rough, but strong-looking. They seemed larger than they should have been. She wore an apron over her bright-colored housedress, and brown leather mules that made a slapping sound every time she walked. She wore her brown, curly hair up in a bun.

My grandmother had a good sense of humor and loved to tell stories. But she was also strong and stern, and that scared me sometimes. It also gave me a real sense of security. I knew that she could be tough if she wanted to and could handle just about anything or anyone. But you could see the warmth in her eyes, too. She taught me you could be strict but show you cared at the same time. Minnie was a motivator. If you did the right thing, she could make you feel ten feet tall, and very, very special.

When I went to spend my summers with her she said, "I have to work all week in my garden and around the house, but once Saturday comes, it will be our special day together. Then Sunday is our day with the Lord." Every Saturday she and I rode in her Model A Ford to downtown Kalamazoo. We always made the five-and-dime store our first stop because that was my favorite place to shop. The dime store was an exciting and friendly place and had everything a seven-year-old could ever want. I especially loved the store's shiny, bright-red store sign, which went nearly the entire length of the building. To me, that friendly sign stood for a good time. Maybe that's why I chose the color red for Wendy's store signs.

I liked to watch the people move from counter to counter, digging through piles of merchandise: Big Ben alarm clocks and Lily-of-the-Valley toilet water, Baby Ruth bars and Cannon towels, Fruit of the Loom shorts, and Lava soap. It was all there.

Then we had lunch at the counter with its swivel seats. I'd order a barbecue sandwich or hot dog or a sloppy joe with a big, big mug of rootbeer. Even then, the people in uniforms making and serving food, hustling back and forth, excited me.

My next stop would be the toy department with its cap guns and toy cars and trucks. Minnie would generally give me some spending money, and often I bought a small toy of some kind.

Our last stop was the candy counter. Grandma would look at me and with a wink would say, "The usual, David?" I didn't say a word, just winked back, and she would tell the clerk, "We'd like one half pound of the bridge mix and one half pound of orange slices, please." I would stuff one of the full, white paper bags, usually the orange slices, into my pocket. She and I would eat up the bridge mix as we wandered through the store.

Some of you are asking, "What's bridge mix?" It's just not as popular today as it was back then. In case you've never heard of it, it's chocolate-coated candy, but in different-sized lumps. It was called bridge mix because society ladies ate it when they played bridge. You never knew what you were biting into when you grabbed a piece—maybe a chocolate-covered raisin, a nut, cream center, or caramel. Of course, when you learned the shapes, it wasn't as much fun. A while back, I told a guy, "They should bring back bridge mix." He snorted and said, "Dave, that'd be like bringing back bow ties." I guess he got me, because all I could say was, "When did THEY go out?"

My grandmother would do some shopping, too. We'd walk by the Simplicity patterns and the J&P Coats sewing threads. Grandma would finger the yard goods in the notions department and say, "They're making this stuff thinner and thinner. They just don't put in the quality like when I was young. Quality's everything, David. Remember that. If people keep cutting corners, this country's going to be in big trouble."

Another thing I admired about my grandmother was that she always seemed to have money. That gave me a good feeling. I don't know how she got it because she lived on a small farm and raised chickens and hogs and grew vegetables. Her house was a two-story double on a dirt road. Minnie's family lived on one side, and she rented the other side out to help make the mortgage payments. The white-painted exterior always looked fresh. Inside, the house had linoleum floors and table tops and a big pot-bellied stove for heating. The cooking stove was electric and the indoor plumbing . . . well, that came later. It was a simple house, but everything was kept neat as a pin.

She managed better than anyone I ever saw. She got so much out of so little, and she never acted poor. Not once did she tell me we couldn't afford something and rarely did I ask her to buy me anything, but I used to dream that I had a lot of money and one day I would take my grandmother to the finest store in town and tell her, "Pick out anything you want, Grandma. Money is no object. Get the best there is with quality that feels expensive!" Later in life, I used to send her money so she could buy the things she would always do without.

My gra__mother was headstrong, too. She was a modern woman, no doubt about it. She always knew what she wanted and went after it. She believed in herself. From the very start, I knew that a woman could do every bit as much as a man, and sometimes more. That's a lesson I learned from Minnie Sinclair.

In my view, all of us owe a special debt to women in their late forties and fifties. Many of these women have helped their husbands, raised families, and put off their own desires. Now they are ready to get going, to do something for themselves. I have worked with a lot of women like this, and they are fantastic. Men can't touch them in terms of drive, desire, and eagerness to work hard. I want these women to know that they're dynamite, and the business world needs them!

Minnie was just that kind of woman. She often said, "You just have to take the bull by the horns." She was independent, as I wanted to be. And she wasn't afraid to show she cared. She taught me some super important lessons. I'm sure she would have agreed with the following suggestions, but I don't know if she would have put them in the same words.

Grandma Minnie's Lessons for Living

1. Make a lot out of a little: Don't waste. Be smart the way you use your time. Do your work in a dependable way.

2. Work hard, and you won't feel so sorry for yourself: Don't sit around and mope. Attend to business. Go out and get something done.

3. Don't cut corners, or you'll sacrifice quality. If you lose quality you lose everything else. People want to get back the quality they see they've lost in the things they buy.

4. Have fun doing things. Decide how you'll divide your time. When you're having fun, focus on having fun. Learn to enjoy your work as much as you can.

5. Be strict but caring, too. Let people know you have values. Let people know you care about them, too.

6. Tackle problems head-on. Don't run away from challenges. Let people know you're going to hang on until something is solved.

7. Pray.

Thirty-five years later, a magazine reporter asked me why Wendy's hamburgers were square. I answered, off the top of my head, "At Wendy's we don't cut corners." It dawned on me then that not cutting corners was a lesson I learned from Minnie Sinclair in "Saturday School" back in Augusta, Michigan.

Grandma Sinclair worked in a restaurant, and she used to help cook the dinner specials, then wash the dishes. The name of the place was Salstrum's. It was located just outside of Augusta. The owner, Mr. Gus Salstrum, had bought an old house and turned it into the favorite restaurant of my youth. When I was about nine, Grandma would sometimes take me to work with her. It was three weeks before I even saw the front of Salstrum's. My grandmother and I had to go in through the back door because only customers were allowed in the front.

One day, though, while Grandma Sinclair was working, I decided to go to the front door and peer inside. I pretended to be a customer. It was a sight inside. There had to be at least fifty tables, all covered with starched white tablecloths and set with silverware that had an "S" engraved on each piece.

Salstrum's had great food. Everything was homemade; Gus even picked his vegetables right out of his garden. Meals were served family-style, and I was impressed at how good the food looked, presented in big round and oblong bowls, pats of butter melting all over the mashed potatoes and green peas as they were carried out of the kitchen. They used to serve gallons and gallons of chicken and dumplings. And they had delicious pastries, which were always swimming in gooey icing.

Most of the time, I would wait in the kitchen. I loved all the hustle and bustle and liked hearing the cook yell at the dishwasher, cursing him for taking too much time. The waitresses would hurry in and out. I had a good feeling there, and I would peek out front at the customers, who were eating, laughing, and having a good time. I could have stayed there all night just watching.

The days I spent with my grandmother were some of the best times of my childhood. The times I spent with my dad were different. He never seemed to be satisfied with the jobs he had, and because of that, we moved around a lot from city to city. Spending the summers with Minnie Sinclair became the one dependable routine in my life, and I looked forward to these times a lot. She seemed to like my being around, but Minnie never liked my adoptive dad. He was working as an auto mechanic around the time my adoptive mother died and would complain about how bored he was with his job. My grandmother didn't want to hear his excuses. They'd argue, and really didn't get along very well. I remember overhearing some of the fights between him and my grandmother before my mother died.

My adoptive father married four times. About seven months after Auleva died, he married a woman named Marie. She was a working woman and had a job in a paper mill; and when she came home at night, the first thing she'd do was pounce on me for not being washed up for dinner. Outside of

Marie's picking on my table manners, she and my dad would ignore me during the whole meal.

Compared with Grandma Minnie, Marie never did anything special for me. In fact, she'd make a point of telling my father when I did something wrong so he would strap me with a belt. She never had children of her own, and maybe she didn't know how to raise kids. Most of the time I didn't know what I did to deserve the licking. I didn't rebel or cause trouble, so I didn't understand why they treated me that way. Maybe Marie and my dad Rex had their own problems. Maybe I had trouble accepting her as my new mother. I don't know, but I was confused.

Rex Thomas was an imposing figure who only had to tell me to do something once. He had a loud, commanding voice, and when he spoke, I knew he meant business. He was tall and muscular—a handsome man, with black hair that he combed straight back. He was a hard worker and honest, but as far as being a father went, he didn't have the time or the inclination. I never remember him hugging me or showing any affection.

I tried to feel proud of him because all kids have a need to look up to their parents, but it wasn't easy. He would build things for the house, and though I'm sure he tried, they always looked sloppy and homemade. Once he built a table, but there was no care in its construction. It was rough-looking and you could see all the nails. I wanted to tell him that if you are going to build something, it should look smooth and professional. Instead, I pretended that I liked it. But I had learned from my grandmother the importance of doing a job right.

After about two and a half years, Dad divorced Marie and we were on our own again. We started going to restaurants for our meals. It was then that I decided I wanted to own my own restaurant because I liked to eat, and I just thought restaurants were really neat, exciting places.

At one point, my dad and I stayed in a rooming house in

Detroit that didn't have a kitchen, so we ate out all the time. Mostly we went to small neighborhood bars and grills that made really good hamburgers and hot dogs. My favorite place was only about six blocks from our apartment and it was strictly a hamburger stand. They'd fry heaps of onions right along with their hamburgers, and the smell alone would make your mouth water. I would always order a hamburger with mustard, pickle, and onion, and the thickest milkshake they could make, one that you had to eat with a spoon. When I founded Wendy's, that was my model for the perfect shake. I worked with chocolate and vanilla ice cream and other ingredients until I came up with just the right taste and smoothness, and I called it a Frosty.

Sometimes we did go to some really nice restaurants, and I was fascinated to see how they served the food. I liked how each restaurant looked different and how they promoted their specials. Some would have really large menus with pictures on them, and some would have tiny handwritten menus, with the blue plate specials done in red. I had definite opinions about each place and whether I wanted to go back or not, based on how things looked and tasted and how friendly the place felt. Most of all, I remember watching families sitting together, having a good time while eating out.

Sure, I liked the food, but the big thing for me was eating out. It was a special event.

When we went out to eat, I had my dad all to myself. Since he went out drinking with his friends a lot in the evenings, dinner was really the only time I had to spend with him. I looked forward to our times out. We didn't talk much, so I would just sit at the counter or table and look around. At the rooming house I didn't get to see many people, just the lady next door who watched me, so I enjoyed seeing new faces and listening to everyone talk and laugh. By the age of nine I had become a real expert on restaurants. I knew what customers expected and I knew what kind of service and quality was acceptable. I overheard complaints and compliments and I soaked them all in.

When World War II broke out, my dad said he was too old to be drafted. It bothered him a little. Mostly, I think it was because he was away from his drinking buddies—who were all in the Army. At the time, he was working in a shipyard in Evansville, Indiana, where he met his third wife, a woman named Viola. They both worked the swing shift. One thing was for sure, Viola was a lot more attractive than Marie. She had a happy personality and was real nice to me. Viola had two daughters from a previous marriage—Dona, who was a little younger than I, and Betty, who was a little older. Because our parents worked such odd hours, Betty and I got ourselves into mischief from time to time. I remember both of us once dressed up like grown-ups and went around the neighborhood, knocking on people's doors to raise money for our church. Since it was dark, nobody looked at us real close. And we really did give the money to the church. So, the first time I put the arm on folks to raise money for a good cause was back when I was ten.

It was a real change for me, going from being alone most of the time to living in a house full of people. Viola said she liked me, but her daughters always seemed to come first. I never got close to my stepsisters because I was always the outsider. I was just a third person, and I never had first pick of anything. It bothered me, but it was better for me to keep my mouth shut if I wanted to stay out of trouble.

There are a lot of kids today in single-parent homes, or who are bounced back and forth between parents in different relationships. That's a real shame, but I know what it feels like, and I can remember what I did that helped steer me through some pretty rough times.

Being a Kid In-Between

1. *Look for people who care about you and learn from them.* For some reason, a Mom or Dad may not be there, or may not be able to help you to learn. Minnie Sinclair filled that role at first for me.

2. *Dream early and build your goals on your dreams.* If I hadn't wanted to run a restaurant when I was eight, I wonder how far I would have gotten. Sure, you can change your dreams, but I think it's real important to have a dream you can live by pretty young in life. It's the best way to keep your energy focused.

3. *Learn to rely on yourself early.* My advice is to keep your eyes on your goal. Work hard toward that goal day by day, minute by minute. It's like an athlete training for the Olympics, practicing every day with that gold medal in sight. In order to be a success you have to really, really want it and believe that you will get it.

4. *If there are things you don't like in the world you grow up in, make your own life different.* I didn't like the way my dad moved around in different jobs, which meant I had to change schools frequently and couldn't make a lot of friends, or how he moved around from marriage to marriage. All these things helped me to establish my own principles. I guess I could have followed the same pattern as my dad, but I decided that I could be different from him. That would never have happened if there had not been other role models around to show me I could do things differently. Fortunately, there were, and I learned from them.

5. *Take a step every day.* I never did anything for pleasure alone. At the end of each day I wanted to say that I developed something or took a step forward. It could be I was too

serious. Certainly, my own five kids and my grandchildren have had fun in their childhood, and that's the way it should be. But, even a young kid can build confidence by seeing himself improve by doing something a little bit better each day.

6. *Be yourself.* I may have been a little more quiet or shy than I should have been, but I was mostly myself, and I didn't worry a lot about trying to be different.

Not too long ago, Dr. Norman Vincent Peale, a great man who wrote the book *The Power of Positive Thinking,* and who recently celebrated his ninety-second birthday, called me up and said that he wanted to feature me in an article in his magazine—*Guideposts.* The theme of the article was "Be Yourself." That was a real compliment. I think that there's a big advantage for business people who follow the principle "Be Yourself." It's this: The more you are comfortable with being yourself, the more time you can spend studying other people. One fellow said about me: "The reason [Dave Thomas has] been such a success is because he has a great sense of people. He knows what they like." If that's true, and I guess it's at least partly true, then it's because I've always tried to pay more attention to other people than to myself.

Paying attention to other people is really important in business. Many young people don't understand big business. It's really about people: how to give them the products they want, how to serve them, how to manage them, how to work with them. Some of the bad reputation business has is deserved. But most business people don't step on others or sleep their way to success. Most companies don't go out of their way to dump garbage in the rivers or to cheat on their income tax. And if it's big, it doesn't mean it's bad. Wendy's is a pretty big company, but we have always tried to let our people be themselves in a positive but natural sort of way.

The article about being yourself was the second time that Dr. Peale had honored me. In 1979, at the Neil House in downtown Columbus, he presented me with the Horatio Alger Award. Meeting Dr. Peale was an honor in itself. He is truly a man of God, a humble man of wisdom, character, and passion. This award really moved me because it recognized what I had done for the free enterprise system. I believe very strongly in free enterprise because it works—and I am living proof. Free enterprise gives every person, regardless of sex, origin, creed, or color, the chance to do something with their lives and to be a success if they are willing to grind it out.

Some people snicker at me and call me a one-man, flag-waving Fourth of July parade, and that is absolutely correct. Let them. I know it works. Most of the Horatio Alger Award recipients came from pretty modest beginnings and made successes of themselves in the business world. Two of my own personal mentors received the award before I did. I was at the luncheon in the Waldorf-Astoria Hotel in New York City when Colonel Harland Sanders, the founder of Kentucky Fried Chicken, got his Horatio Alger Award. In 1968, I was invited to be there when another friend and advisor of mine, Kenny King, President of Kenny King's Family Restaurants, received the Alger Award. Through hard work, a burning desire, and integrity, these two men had pulled themselves up by their bootstraps. I never thought that they would be honoring me this way.

The *Today Show* had me as a guest. Plenty of newspapers and magazines interviewed me. The Horatio Alger Association elected me its president for two years, and I spoke to twelve thousand high school students all over the U.S. and told them they didn't need to be born with silver spoons in their mouths. Get rid of the "I-don't-think-I-can" attitude, I said, and believe in "I know I can," because it's true. Maybe my story encouraged one or two others. If it did, then all the talks were worth it. A lot of young people have lost faith in the American Way, and I think the only way to win them back is to give them the hard facts about how you can succeed.

Today, I do plenty of public speaking and appear in lots of TV commercials, but when I was young I was a shy kid. You wouldn't call me shy today, but people say that I'm soft-spoken. Overcoming my shyness helped me achieve what I did later. Here are a couple of things I picked up on dealing with my shyness that really helped me out.

Getting Over Shyness

1. *Don't think too much about what other people think about you.* One of the reasons people are shy is that they don't want to take risks; they don't want to be rejected by someone else. It's more important that you like yourself than for everybody in the world to like you. So, don't worry so much over what other people think about you. If you don't take any chances, you'll never be able to really make friends with anybody.

2. *Find something to do that gets you around people.* For me, that was getting into the restaurant business. For others, it's sports or 4-H or the Scouts. The key is to spend more time with other people. Once you do, the shyness will melt away.

3. *Make friends one at a time.* Some people try to become really social over night. That just doesn't work. The best way to get over being shy is to build your friendships one at a time.

4. *Look for people who think like you do.* Over time, you want to be comfortable with all kinds of people—some who agree with you and some who don't. But, in general, you're better off starting out to make friends with people who share your views than with people who are really different.

5. *Get in touch with the feelings that cause you to be shy.* Do you think that people think you act or look funny? Are you afraid people don't think you are good enough to be a friend? Are you afraid that you will stumble around or sound dumb when you talk? If you can put your finger on what exactly you're afraid of, of what exactly makes you shy, you can start to do something about it . . . and find out that your fear isn't really so scary after all.

Sometimes, I still clutch up before a heavy-duty public appearance. When President Bush asked me to be a national spokesperson for the "Adoption Works . . . For Everyone" campaign, that meant I had to make some comments to the Washington press corps. This was a great honor, but when I saw the twenty microphones and the fifty people, did I start to sweat! To get over the fear, I just made myself believe that I was talking to one or two of my closest friends, and everything was a breeze.

It's easy to get over shyness if you muster the courage and take one little risk at a time. When you do, you'll be surprised at how many people out there really want to be your friend.

2

Starting From Scratch

Since my house was never a really pleasant place to be, I decided to try to get a job. My older stepsister worked and seemed to gain respect for bringing home money. So, when I was ten years old, I got my first job at a filling station in Princeton, Indiana. Some old guy hired me to watch the station for him a couple of hours a day so he could eat his lunch. The station only had two gas pumps, so I just hung around with not much to do. I don't even remember if he paid me, but it was a place to go to get out of the house during the summer.

Paper routes were a popular job for kids then, so I gave that a try next. I had the afternoon route and I remember really hating it. I had to fold each paper and I had to collect, but the hardest part was finding the right houses because the addresses were confusing. I had nobody to help me or show me what to do, so I just quit. Then I was a golf caddy. That didn't work, either. I went on to be a pinsetter in a bowling alley, but I hated that. After one week in that noisy, dirty bowling alley, I thought it was a zero deal and quit. I thought a lot about working in a restaurant, but every place I went they said I was just too young. So I was forced to put my real ambition on hold for two years.

In the summer of 1944, my family moved from Indiana to Knoxville, Tennessee, where my dad found work as a supervisor on a construction site making good money, he said. That justified moving again. The jobs he held in Tennessee were all part of the construction boom that happened when the country's first nuclear reactor was built in Oak Ridge, Tennessee. I was twelve years old then, and this was my fourth move in six years. I didn't get to know many kids in Indiana, but I did know a few from school and I missed them. Now I had to face the struggle of trying to meet new friends. I wasn't up for it, so for three days I just slept late and moped around. My dad had enough of that and told me to go out and get a job. The next day I wandered out of our house down to the main street of town and noticed a Help Wanted sign in a grocery store window.

Why not? I was sure they wouldn't hire a twelve-year-old, but since I was big for my age, I decided I would say I was fifteen. I hate lying, and I have never tolerated it in business. But I figured I had to stand up for myself. "Don't tell me I'll be last in line for everything anymore. Beginning right now, I'll make my own deal," I said to myself.

The grocery store was small and every inch of space was crammed full of boxes, bags, and cans of food. I told the older man behind the counter—Dave—I was fifteen. Dave said he'd try me out and told me I'd be cleaning up around the store and delivering groceries when there was need for it. I said I was strong enough to handle it. My pay was 20 cents an hour and a sandwich for lunch. I started at eight sharp in the morning, when I'd sweep the sidewalk in front of the store, and worked until 4 P.M. Delivering groceries in hilly Knoxville is no fun. I delivered on a bike, and it seemed that every one of my customers lived in an apartment house on the top of a steep hill. When I got off the bike at the top of the hill and read the building mail boxes, one customer after another turned out to live on the fourth or fifth floor. After a couple weeks of that, I had leg muscles like a mountain goat.

To motivate myself, I thought about the money that I would be earning on my own, and I had fun trying to decide how I was going to spend it. I had a new bike in mind, but Dave called me aside after about four weeks. He said I'd done a good job but that he was closing the store for two weeks so he could go on vacation. In a way, I was happy to hear the news. It was really hot, and I could spend some time at the rec center swimming pool nearby. Then, a week later, Dave called and said he came back early and wanted me back in on Monday. On the phone, I stammered and said, since he told me I'd be off for two weeks, I'd already made some plans. When I didn't show up the next Monday, the Help Wanted sign went back up in the window, and I knew I was fired. Every now and then I can close my eyes and see that sign in my mind. It's sort of a symbol for a lesson I learned from the experience: When you take a job, you better be ready to show up for work when it suits your boss . . . not just when it suits you.

The next week, I applied for work at a Walgreen's Drug Store. I had to lie about my age again in order to get the job. I told the manager I was sixteen. I worked behind the soda fountain with another guy who said that I learned real fast. It was lots of fun mixing sodas and making ice-cream floats and sundaes. I really liked wearing the Walgreen's uniform of white pants and a black bow tie. I felt special behind that counter, taking orders and making change. It was my first restaurant job and I loved it.

I worked at Walgreen's for about three weeks when the manager began to get suspicious about my age. One day I asked him if I could have permission to have several days off because I had to travel with my family. It made me look like I wasn't old enough to stay home and take care of myself. He started asking me a lot of questions, and when I admitted the truth, they stopped scheduling me. For a part-timer, not getting scheduled is the silent-treatment version of getting fired.

I'll never forget my dad's face when I told him I'd lost my job at Walgreen's. I thought he would understand about the age and all, but he didn't. He got so angry I thought the veins in his neck would burst. "I know about the grocery store job, too, David. I checked and they told me you refused to show up for work and got fired." He slammed his fist on the kitchen table and screamed, "You'll never keep a job! I'll be supporting you for the rest of your life!"

I can tell you that moment has stayed with me, and I vowed to myself, "I'll never lose another job again."

Determined to find work again, I set out one day in downtown Knoxville. I saw a sign in the large front window of the Regas Restaurant, and I decided this was the place for me. The Regas wasn't fancy, but everything was polished to a looking-glass shine. The National Restaurant Association membership sign over the counter was hung with such pride, you'd think that some guide book had just pasted five stars on the owner's forehead. I sold myself hard to a man named Mr. Briscoe. Since I was still new to Knoxville, I didn't know what a great reputation the Regas had. I just saw this nice-looking restaurant with brown wood trim, and thought it looked like a good place to work. When Mr. Briscoe asked me why I wanted a job, I told him that I loved the restaurant business. I also told him I was sixteen, although I was really twelve.

Little did brothers Frank and George Regas, owners of the Regas Restaurant, know they had the youngest counterman in the state on their payroll. But I was in the restaurant business again. I was right where I wanted to be.

There were seventeen stools at the Regas lunch counter

where I worked along with Bill Regas, Frank's son, who was four years older than I. Bill himself went on to be an important person in the restaurant industry. Bill and I worked well together, a real team. You'd never have known that he was the boss's son. We all stood on our own merits. Looking back at an old snapshot, I think Bill and I looked pretty sharp in our gray smock coats, crisp white aprons, white shirts, and ties. I felt very professional in my uniform. We draped towels over our left arms to wipe up spills and keep the counters spotless. We weren't allowed to use serving trays, so I had to learn how to balance plates, cups and saucers, and carry everything by hand. The big challenge was to carry four plates of food and multiple cups of coffee at the same time without dripping or spilling anything. If you could do that, you were a success. Also, all orders were taken by memory, and checks were made out the same way. We often had a hundred customers in a single night.

At that time, 1944, a meal at the Regas, such as a meat loaf plate, was 40 cents, 45 cents with dessert. Eggs, any style, were 20 cents, and coffee was a nickel. My salary then was 25 cents an hour, but some days I would make as much as $5.00 in tips.

During the summer, I worked at the Regas every day. During the school year, I worked every weekend. The Regas was open twenty-four hours a day, and I worked the twelve-hour shift from 8 P.M. to 8 A.M. Gene Rankin, a Regas brother-in-law who was also one of my managers, and I used to start cleaning up at 2 A.M., and then we'd make egg, ham, and tuna sandwiches for the next day. Sometimes we'd make up as many as four hundred sandwiches a night. This was during World War II, and everybody working back home tried to give a little extra on the job. This work style set a standard for me. I became used to putting out a lot of volume when I was very young; I just thought that it was the way you were supposed to do it. If somebody pays you, it was up to you to perform.

Breakfast service began at 4 A.M. After making sandwiches, I would work until eight in the morning, go home, fall into bed, and sleep until about three in the afternoon.

Mr. Frank and his brother, George Regas, were real influences in my life. Perhaps Frank saw a little of himself in me. Born in Patras, Greece, in 1888, Frank came to America because he couldn't get along with his stepmother. He borrowed $100 from his father and traveled over on a steamer when he was fifteen. He didn't have a job and couldn't speak English. He found work as a $20-a-month dishwasher and paid his father back as soon as he could. In his first dishwashing job, he would be on duty twenty-four hours straight. He would nap on a cot, and they would haul him down whenever they needed the dishes washed. He hated it, but it really lit a fire under him to get ahead. He got a job as a cook for $15 a week and paid another cook $5.00 to teach him how to make meat loaf and beef stew. I admired Frank because he was both so tough and so fair. He used to say, "As long as you try, you can do anything you want to do, be anything you want to be." I believed him.

Frank Regas was short and stocky and full of energy. He would come to work every day in a three-piece suit. He loved to wear a vest with a pocket watch, but when the crowds started coming through the door he would take off his jacket, roll up his sleeves, and pitch in wherever help was needed. There's nothing he wouldn't do in the restaurant. He'd bus dishes or even wash dishes . . . whatever it took. Frank liked to wear a suit, but he used to say that you didn't have to wear a suit or expensive clothes to make a good impression. But he would look for people that were clean and took pride in themselves, especially when he was hiring. If they did that much, he felt, they would take pride in their work.

George Regas was a hard worker who started out running a hot dog stand. He was a proud man who was generous with his praise. He really tried to build a sense of family in all of the Regas employees. He cared about us as people and helped us to work together as a team.

The Regas brothers believed in and demanded cleanliness and quality. If you touched a butter patty with your fingers, you could be fired. They valued each and every customer and told us that we were there because of the customer, and that it was our job to keep them coming back. "If you give poor service and lose a customer," Mr. Frank used to say, "don't try to alibi by saying that it was only one customer. I won't buy it. Work as if your job depends on every single customer, every day, because it does."

Frank Regas stood up for the employees, too. I once saw him ask a customer to leave the restaurant when he insulted one of our waiters. Another time, a drunk came in and started harassing the girls, and Mr. Frank took him by the seat of his pants and threw him right out in the street. "No hard-working man or woman should be called names and treated like a dog," he said.

Every Saturday when Gene Rankin and I sat down to eat, I talked to him about someday opening my own business. He told me, "There's a lot of opportunity out there and you'll make a lot of money, but you have to set high goals and work hard to achieve them." Gene was the first person to hear about my dream of owning a restaurant.

I used to get awful tired working twelve hours a day, and I was glad that I didn't have far to go when my shift was over since we lived only about ten blocks from the restaurant. But then, about six months later, I got some bad news. My father got a new job as a pipefitter, this time in Oak Ridge itself. After he tried commuting for a while, he finally decided the family had to move closer to his work. My dad knew I loved my own job, but there was no way he could or would drive me sixty miles a day, so he gave me a choice. Either I quit my job at the Regas and find another one in Oak Ridge, or I could ride the Trailways bus to and from work every day. I only had to think about it for a minute.

During the school year, I rode the bus back and forth to Knoxville on the weekends. When summer came, I convinced my dad to let me rent a sleeping room close to the restaurant. I was almost fourteen and excited about the chance to be on my own. He agreed, as long as I could pay the rent—which was $7.00 a week. My pay was pretty good and I was confident I could handle things on my own. At least I'd be calling all my own shots.

I didn't have any hobbies or special interests. There was just no time for things like that. There was no TV, either. Once in a while, when I did get a night off, I'd go to the show, as the movies were called back then. Cowboy pictures and serials were my favorite, and Gene Autry and Roy Rogers were my heroes. They were honest and patriotic, and I respected them. Even though I was doing what I wanted to do, between work and school, my schedule was starting to wear me down.

One night, when I was real tired, I broke down and told Gene Rankin the truth, that I had just turned fourteen. I was physically tired, but most of all I was tired of having lied to the people at the Regas who had done so much to give me a chance. Gene said that everyone there suspected I wasn't sixteen. "But you had such determination," he said, "we just decided to let it go."

I went ahead working at the Regas for another four months until my family moved back to Indiana. On my last day of work, Frank Regas took me aside and talked to me man to man. "If you ever come back and want a job, it's yours," he said.

What the Regas experience taught me really stuck with me through my entire career, especially when I founded Wendy's. The number one thing they taught me was motivation. Every day either Gene or one of the Regas brothers would pat me on the back and tell me I was doing a good job. When I made a mistake, instead of calling me on the carpet for it, they would first point out something good that I had done, and then they would explain what I had done wrong and show me how to correct my mistake. They never criticized me or made me feel small in front of anyone. "Everyone makes mistakes, David," they'd say. They made sure I'd learn from the mistakes without losing my drive and still keep an upbeat attitude. Their formula is working today. The Regas Restaurant in Knoxville is still one of the best restaurants in America.

If I had to summarize what I learned at the Regas, my list would look something like this:

The Regas Rules for Restaurants

- Make a clean, neat impression—it doesn't have to be fancy—and you take step number one in this business.
- Do everything you can to keep customers happy. Your job really depends on their coming back.
- Set tough standards ("Don't touch the butter patties!") because customers set tough standards.
- Back your employees when the situation calls for it.
- Build your people's confidence. Tell them what they are doing right, and make it easy for them to learn from their mistakes.
- Reward motivation and determination in the people who work on your team.
- Try—really try—and you can do anything you want to.

It was 1947 when my dad moved the family to Fort Wayne, where he had found a job as a steamfitter at U.S. Rubber. Although the move put us only a hundred miles from my grandmother, whom I really missed, it also put us all into a house trailer. It may have been a big trailer, but there were six of us cramped into it, and one of them was a baby named Pat—born to Viola and my dad. There wasn't much privacy and no indoor toilet.

It was really rough going back to living with the family every day. I had had a taste of independence in Knoxville and I wanted it again. The key for me was finding a new job. In the help-wanteds, a new restaurant was opening up and the manager was looking for people, including a busboy. It was the Hobby House Restaurant on East Wayne Street. I put on my best clothes to make the best impression I could, even though the job was as a busboy. The manager of the Hobby House was a gruff-looking but friendly man named Ralph Warren. He hired me on the spot because he said he liked my attitude. I told him I would be the best busboy he ever had.

After the interview I noticed a man dressed in a suit sweeping the floor and stopping every now and then to clear off placemats and wipe up the tan Formica tables after customers left. I thought that was peculiar and almost asked Ralph if that was how the crew dressed around here, but I kept a lid on it.

My hourly wage was 50 cents, but I got a nickel raise after only the first week. I made up my mind to work as hard as I could and get promoted to the fountain. The Hobby House was basically a short-order coffee shop with food at popular prices. It seated about 150 people and guaranteed really fast service, so I had to be on the ball. After about four weeks, I got on the fountain, and I really enjoyed making the banana splits, sundaes, and milkshakes I had learned about at Walgreen's. My eye was on the front kitchen, though, because I could make more money working there, and I would learn a lot, too. If I was going to own a restaurant, I wanted to know how to do everyone's job.

A month later, when school let out for summer vacation, Ralph told me he'd let me go in the kitchen and work, and he raised my pay to $35 a week for fifty hours or more. The hard work was paying off. I felt good about myself and about my work, and I was feeling real close to the other people who worked there. They were becoming like a family to me. They cared about me and seemed interested in my opinions and how I felt about things.

We were busiest when summer came, and I began working a lot of hours. I was working on the steam table, grill, french fryer, and sandwich table. I was racking up a lot of overtime, but it wasn't showing up in my checks, so I decided to see the bookkeeper. In the bookkeeper's office, there was the man in the suit, the same guy I saw sweeping floors and bussing dishes when I started. "Hi," he said, "I'm Phil Clauss—the owner of the Hobby House." What a shock.

Phil took care of the overtime problem. More important, every week after that, he would take a few minutes to talk to me. He was a nice man, a hard worker, and an innovator who believed in progress and changes. He really meant a lot to me. He was becoming like a father to me.

Phil really motivated me and believed that it was plenty more important to do something than to do nothing. If Phil had a problem (yes, mentors don't always do everything right), it was hard for him to step back and look at the big picture. He was pitching in so much that sometimes he didn't organize things as much as he should have. Also, he had a hard time with delegation. He really tried, but couldn't always do it right. His personal instinct for taking care of the customer was so strong, he sometimes made you feel you might as well close the door because you could never do it as well as he did. When he went on vacation, you got the message: "Do the best you can till I get back." But, everything considered, he was a great teacher.

Phil had lots of energy, and was always doing lots of different things. Whatever he did got attention. If he was doing pancakes, he was the best pancake maker you ever met. Phil was also the kind of guy who said, "If I can do it, anybody can do it." I used to try to match hour to hour with him.

Toward the end of summer, my adoptive dad told me the family had to move again. This time I had no reason to go with them. I had a job, I had my own family at the restaurant, and I had already learned from my adoptive grandmother that I was adopted.[2] There was no way I was leaving Fort Wayne.

The YMCA was about a block from the Hobby House, and they rented me a room. When I told my dad I was staying in Fort Wayne, he didn't seem surprised by my decision, but I think he was surprised at how determined I was. I didn't ask him if it was O.K.; I just told him this was what I intended to do.

I remember he was packing his tools outside the trailer, getting ready for the move. "Someday you'll be proud of me," I said, choking up. "I'm going to have my own restaurant, and I'm going to be a success." "I hope you're right, son," he said. "Good luck to you." That was all he said. That was the end of it. After that, I didn't see him for three years. We sent Christmas cards to each other and talked on the phone once or twice, but I didn't see him again until I left for the Army.

---

[2]Later in this book, I will tell you about my adoption and how it affected me. No doubt about it, being adopted has had a big influence on the way I have looked at life and why I have made adoption a personal crusade. It's such a big deal that I don't want to sidetrack you by getting into the details here.

What I did is not something I'd recommend to any kid today. I was fifteen years old, working fifty hours a week minimum, still in Fort Wayne Central High, and living at the Y. It wasn't much longer—in fact, just after I finished the tenth grade—before I quit school. I'd learned reading and writing, but my real vocation was the restaurant business, and school wasn't teaching me what I wanted to know. Plenty of schools do a better job today with vocational training. If that had been true when I was in school, maybe I would have stuck it out.

I remember writing an essay in tenth grade called "The Pursuit of Happiness" that was published in *The Spotlight,* Central's school paper. In it, I wrote, "Do the work you like to do. You maybe could earn more money by being the president of the company, but would you be happy? You would be better off being a truck driver than you would being the president of the company if you like driving trucks best . . ." I also wrote: "Before I ever go into business for myself, I am going to know my business. I am going to start on a small scale and build my business and my experience together.

"After I finish school, I want to join the Army for a while and be a cook. In this way, I will be getting more experience. I will have my education and my Army experience. I will be all set to start the pursuit of happiness with a restaurant of my own."

Except for not finishing high school, that was my strategic plan, and I achieved it all. My plan wasn't fancy, but it was all that I needed. For some reason, my teacher actually kept the paper. Unbeknownst to me, she would read it over the years to her classes. The writing itself wouldn't win any prizes, but she thought it was surprising for a tenth-grader to have such a clear idea of what he wanted to do. Maybe the reason that my plan worked was that it was so simple and that it zeroed in on the skills I had to have . . . not on making a lot of dough.

After I dropped out of school, I began to feel more and more lonely. I was working every day now from morning till night. I started to miss the change of pace school provided. Phil Clauss and I were getting closer than ever and he could tell I was feeling low. He suggested that I leave the YMCA and go to live with his sister, Esther Marquart, and her husband, Lloyd. They had two daughters and a son, and he thought I would be happier living with a family, having a home and people to return to every night.

They were wonderful people, and some of my happiest times were spent with them. I gave them a token amount of money for rent, and they gave me something money can't buy—a sense of belonging. Esther says that I was fun-loving, and that I liked to debate things in a cheerful way. Maybe. I only know that the family feeling I had with them and the family feeling of the Hobby House restaurant were stronger than the family I had known at "home."

My future goal was to become manager of the Hobby House, but the Korean War started and I knew I would be drafted. So in 1950, with Phil's blessing and a promise that I would always have a job, I joined the Army. My dad had to give special approval because I was only seventeen when I signed up.

When I look at this particular time in my life, what looms largest was that I was young *and* on my own. I made it through O.K., but there are plenty of kids who aren't so lucky. Maybe I stumbled onto some things that made it easier for me. Anyway, here are some of the beliefs I ended up with that helped pull me through.

Dave's Plan for Making It
If You're Young,
Alone, and on Your Own

1. *Get a job.* My adoptive dad was right, although the way
he made me feel when he said I'd never be able to hold a job
was pretty harsh. Even though they weren't on their own, all
five of my kids got jobs pretty early. Three of them worked for
Wendy's. Pam actually helped train some of the first managers we hired to work at Wendy's. Kenny worked in the restaurant and became an early franchisee. Molly worked in the
restaurants and in our headquarters. Wendy didn't work behind the counter (except at the Wendy's tent at the Ohio State
Fair), but she, of course, has been an ambassador for the
company since its beginning. Lori was too young to work at
Wendy's in the early days, but when she was old enough, she
got a job working in a fashion clothing store. I think that
working helped build a sense of responsibility in the kids.
Even if the job is simple and the family as a whole is earning
a good income, a job can give you plenty of satisfaction and
pride that goes beyond money.

Kids today have it a lot tougher. There are so many distractions. It's easy to sit on your duff watching MTV. It would
probably have been that way for me, too, but it's hard for me
to imagine what Glenn Miller would have looked like on
MTV.

2. *Don't be discouraged if an early job doesn't work out.* I
was fired from or quit my first six jobs. When you start out,
you're still learning about life. If you make the first job you
ever have your career, you could be lucky . . . or you could not
be asking yourself tough enough questions about what you
really want.

3. *Look for things you like, and learn what it takes to have them.* I really liked the uniforms, the shiny registers, and the bustle of the restaurant business. But you also have to be willing to put up with the work that goes behind the nice things. In my business, that meant the long hours, the hot kitchens, and the cleaning up. To do most jobs well, you have to work hard. Lots of young people want to be actresses or rock stars, but they don't know all the grunt work that it takes to be really good in those jobs, and there's plenty of it.

4. *Try hard work.* I can hear all those groans right now, but I still remember those twelve-hour shifts when I was fourteen and making four or five hundred sandwiches at two in the morning. You end up exhausted, but the sense of accomplishment you get is a real high.

5. *Find people you can learn from.* Boy, was I lucky to get a one-two punch like the Regas Brothers and then Phil Clauss! But there are plenty of classy people out there who want to help. Instead of just waiting for somebody to take you under their wing, go out there and find a good wing to climb under.

6. *Get an education.* I didn't follow my own advice, and I still regret it today. There's no way in today's world that I could have done what I did without a better education. That's because the restaurant industry, and nearly every other business, is a whole lot more professional. You have to understand systems management and finance or your chances are pretty slim.

7. *Figure out what the bottom is.* If you can envision the worst thing that can happen to you and you think you can still handle it, then you might have a shot. In fact, if you prepare yourself for the worst, you'll probably do better than you expect.

3

Join the Army and Become an Entrepreneur

I reported for my Army basic training at eighteen. Like a lot of people, I joined up to get an education. The Korean War was about to start, and I've always been pretty patriotic, but I didn't say to myself, "Gee, I love my country, and I have to do my duty." I also didn't sign up to make up for my dad, who never served. I enlisted because I knew I would be drafted sooner or later, and back then, if you enlisted, you had a better chance of choosing your specialty. I was also ready for a new, fresh experience. The Hobby House was good to me, but I had learned most everything I could and it was getting time to move on.

My enlistment marked the beginning of a long and important relationship between me and the U.S. Armed Forces. I'm proud to be a life member of the American Legion Post 411 in Dublin, Ohio—although I'm the first to admit that the closest I ever got to battlefield conflict was dirty looks from GIs on the other side of a chow line. On the last Veteran's Day, Wendy's signs all over the country read: "America is No. 1 thanks to our veterans." We really believe that. But the service can also be a good deal for an individual as well as the country, provided you have the right attitude.

Dave's Six Tips on Serving Yourself While Serving Your Country—Or Anyone/Anything Else

1. Don't be afraid to volunteer.

2. Take a little initiative.

3. Make your own job bigger.

4. Mine the "gold" out of the garbage.

5. Find ways to be an entrepreneur.

6. Help improve morale.

1. *Don't be afraid to volunteer.* People tell you not to volunteer for anything when you're in the service. That's just plain dumb.

My basic training tour began in October 1950 at Fort Benning, Georgia. During my first week, my teeth started to give me real trouble, and the company dentist had to do a root canal operation. I could hardly open my mouth because my jaws were so swollen and sore. I couldn't eat and could barely talk. The dentist wrote me out a medical release saying that I was benched from basic training for at least ten days, until the infection cleared up.

I started to get bored from sitting around with nothing to do. Not one to stay in bed, I went down to the mess hall and volunteered to work there until they would let me back into basic. I guess that I was curious, too, about how the Army ran its version of a restaurant. Just how did such a big operation work? For the next few weeks, I cleared tables, swept up, and helped the cooks a little.

Some thought my gung-ho attitude was a bit weird. But I figured that I knew something about feeding people, and I could turn this into an edge. My gut instincts were right; there were some staffing problems in the mess hall. Some of the cooks were "lifers" who were just re-upping themselves to get their twenty-year pension. They would get drunk and wouldn't show up for work. That meant I got involved in cooking more and more.

Finally, the mess hall sergeant asked me if I wanted to go to Cook and Baker's School. He said it was too late for me to get back into basic training since I had missed already so much. Forget about fifty-pound backpacks and midnight drills in the Georgia swamps, I said to myself. For a second time, I volunteered real fast! It didn't break my heart that I wouldn't be able to complete basic training.

Cook and Baker's School was an eight-week course. We worked twenty-four hours cooking dinner, breakfast, lunch, and then dinner again, and then we were off for twenty-four hours. I learned to cook a few new things, but mostly we were taught measuring and quantity systems. I wasn't very good at the baking side of it and hated it. You've got to have patience to be a baker, and that's not my thing. Overall, the school gave me some important skills about the big picture of feeding a lot of people—skills I was glad to have later.

2. *Take even a little initiative, and it'll improve your odds.* During the eighth week of school, word came down that my division was getting ready to ship out to either Korea or Germany. This was four years after the end of World War II, and Germany was still a pile of rubble. Korea had been a shooting war (or should I say "police action"?) for just a few months. Most of us in the outfit were hoping we would go to Germany. My commanding officer came to school and told me that I would be going to Germany on Sunday. Then he

shocked the heck out of me as he said, "Corporal Thomas, you're now a sergeant," and gave me my stripes.

Being a staff sergeant at the age of eighteen was quite an honor, and getting promoted was very exciting. Did· volunteering get me there? Partly. When a division shipped out overseas, every slot on the table of the organization had to be filled. They needed just so many captains, corporals, and so on. There was a vacancy for a sergeant, which I hadn't even known about. But because I had made an impression on someone who was scrambling to fill a slot, I got picked for the job. A little initiative will improve your luck nine days out of ten.

Even better, I was assigned to Division Headquarters, which is a good place to be if your name isn't Rambo and you weren't born with a bayonet between your teeth. That suited me. A food manager would probably learn more by being around a commanding general than some field outpost, I thought, and I was right. No Hollywood screenwriter could ever dream up a name like my commanding general's, though. His honest-to-God name was General Harland Hartless. Cross my heart!

In the spring of 1951 we sailed for Germany. The Army barracks in Frankfurt, which were built by the Germans during World War II, were really large, spacious, and well ventilated. Frankly, they were better than those in the States.

3. *Make your own job bigger.* I was a cook in the consolidated mess halls, where we fed up to two thousand people a day. It was hard work for the people on the line. I had three men under my command, but since the routine never changed, things were getting monotonous, especially since my workers didn't need much supervising.

Rather than waiting for a new assignment, I began looking around for ways to make my own job more·interesting. Plenty of people complain that they are bored stiff with their job, but they don't do anything about it. They don't look for ways to make their job more challenging. I began to think: "What problem is there in this operation that I could help fix?" There *was* one big problem: There was a lot of stuff the mess hall needed but couldn't get. Anybody who could help solve that problem would be sure to get ahead.

If you needed new pots or silverware you had to turn in your used, battered ones for new. If you didn't have any used stuff to turn in, someone had to pay for new things, and it was the mess hall officer and the company commander who had to come up with the money out of their budgets. Needless to say, we did without a lot of things. I began trying to make some deals, and that was the beginning of my new "job."

4. *Mine the "gold" out of the garbage.* There's always been an incredible amount of waste in the Armed Services because nobody's accountable. Things have gotten a lot better in recent years, but you can often find things as good as gold in a government-issue dumpster. The Air Force mess staff would often just throw away their beat-up utensils and tableware. I used to go to the dump and take the things my outfit could use. Then we would either turn around and trade it in for new, or we would use it.

After I did this a few times, my mess officer began to be impressed with the money I was saving him. He would send me out to "scrounge" for specific items. I had his permission to use the general's jeep, and I would go out trading with other units. They needed forks; we were knee-deep in forks but needed potholders. We needed paprika; they were waist-high in paprika but needed gaskets for their pressure cookers. It was like Monte Hall and "Let's Make a Deal."

Now, I didn't sneak around in the dead of night and just take things. I wrote up hundreds of requisitions that sometimes paid off and sometimes were ignored. When requisitioning didn't work, I would just try to make some contacts or hang out around the trading sites. That way, I used the downtime from my job to get ahead.

5. *Find ways to be an entrepreneur.* Instead of thinking like a lowly mess sergeant, I was really thinking and acting like an entrepreneur—taking risks, making deals, and creating value in unexpected places. The military can be one of the best places in the world to learn to be an entrepreneur. Any place with plenty of rules—rules that sometimes conflict with each other or are hard to enforce—will reward people who get around those rules in a way that doesn't harm the organization or the people in it.

I was slowly making a name for myself. The company commander, mess officer, and mess sergeant really liked what I was doing. They made me their underground, unofficial procurement officer. Their permission and their vote of confidence was all that I needed.

6. *Help improve morale.* My big project was to get some paint for the mess halls. Everybody was complaining about how dingy the mess halls looked, but nobody had the guts to say we needed paint. The mess halls got painted every five years, and though it had only been two years, the place looked terrible. I felt that the troops deserved better, and a little paint wasn't asking too much.

I first went to the officer in charge of engineering. He said, "No way. They were just painted a few years ago." While I was walking out of his office I overheard a phone conversation about some colonel's wife who needed paint for her house. The clerk handling the call ok'd it.

I charged back into his office and told the officer what I had just heard. I said, "Sir, our men are here serving their country and the colonel's wife is only serving cookies and tea." He got real huffy and barked, "Regulations prohibit me from authorizing paint for the mess halls."

I was really mad by this time and decided I would get that paint if it took me the rest of my duty tour. I talked to everyone I could. I raised hell about it and put in requisitions all over the place. Finally, I don't know which requisition hit or who saw it through for me, but one day I got a truckload of five hundred gallons of paint.

Rarely have I ever enjoyed being a big shot, but this time I did. I was really big, someone important: I was the only one who had the paint. My rank or time-in-grade didn't matter. Suddenly and somehow, I had gotten control of something that would improve morale in a big way . . . and, in the Army, that is real power.

When I presented the paint to my mess hall sergeant, my reputation turned to gold. Each company was evaluated on appearance, and after we painted the mess halls and the barracks, we got a high rating. Most important, the troops were proud. You could tell by the way they walked and joked when they came in for chow. There was less griping, and fewer jokes about "s——t on a shingle"—that Army staple of chipped beef on toast. I learned the power of a simple coat of paint, and it's a lesson we have repeated countless times since to motivate employees and help make customers happier in our Wendy's restaurants.

The paint story also had a moment of sweet revenge to it. The engineering officer who refused my paint request came to me. He wanted to paint his office and asked for three gallons of my paint. I was real diplomatic and told him, "No, sir. I just wouldn't feel right about that. The men of this division have fought awful hard to get this paint. I'm afraid you'll have to go and do your own deal and put in your requisition just like I did."

● ● ●

When I think back about my Army experience, one thing is clear to me: If you use your head, you can really serve yourself while you serve your country. That's what I tried to do when I was in the Army.

When I did these things—and partly because of the way I did these things—the Army and the soldiers I was really working for all benefited. These were things that truly helped the Army organization. So, while I was serving myself, what I did wasn't self-serving in the sense that it wasn't done just for me. Also, in my opinion, these rules can help anyone in military service or civilian life. I don't care if you are a man or a woman, in the U.S. Coast Guard, the Norwegian Navy, or most civilian jobs.

The Army taught me some other things later on that had more to do with my particular specialty—building a food-service business. My roommate, Master Sergeant Ed McCauley, managed the Enlisted Men's Club. Mac and I talked a lot about the Club's kitchen business. They were only doing $40 a day on food and I had ideas on how he could boost sales. The GIs really came to the Club to drink; but if they had wanted to eat the food, prices were sure cheap enough. Sandwiches were priced at a quarter, and you could get a full meal for under a dollar. I volunteered to go to the Club at night and help out. This was the third piece of smart volunteering for me, and it really paid off again.

Sergeant McCauley was a tough forty-year-old Irishman, and a close personal friend of General Hartless. They served in combat together in the Pacific. Mac was a hard worker and I really admired him. When my suggestions started paying off, he came to respect my judgment, and he knew I was honest and loyal. Mac had an assistant who was about to be discharged. He said he needed someone willing to work hard. "I want you. Do you want the job?" he asked.

I was thrilled. "Yeah," I said. "I'd love it, but I don't think I can get it."

Being an assistant manager at the Club was a prestigious job, and you got paid $75.00 extra a month. No young kid eighteen years old ever got a job like that. You had to be a career soldier or in the service at least twenty years.

"Listen," Mac said, "you just go to your company commander and request permission to be transferred to the Club." He sent me to see my commander, and I didn't have to say a word. He stood up, came out from behind his desk, and shook my hand. "Congratulations," he said. "You are now assigned to work with Sergeant McCauley at the Enlisted Men's Club."

I found out later that if Sergeant McCauley wanted anything he just went to his friend the general. And he wanted me. I was grateful to Sergeant McCauley for his trust and I told him I wouldn't let him down. When anybody gives me their trust, I make sure that I thank them. You can bet that in 1972, when the first twenty investors each kicked in $50,000 to bankroll Wendy's first expansion, I said plenty of "thank-yous." Trust is about the most valuable thing anyone can give you in business, and you can never show too much appreciation for it.

My whole focus was on building up the food business. It might sound pretty dull, being an assistant manager at an enlisted men's club, but that's not how I see it today. Working at the Club was my first opportunity to build and turn around a restaurant operation that was flat on its back. And because it was a government facility and didn't have any shareholders, I was able to take risks without having to mortgage my house or be afraid I'd lose my job overnight.

Basically, I just did things that made common sense. For example, they were just serving cold sandwiches when I got there. They obviously forgot that most of their customers were guys in their late teens and early twenties, guys who liked a nice snack at night. But these boys didn't want a fancy REST-AU-RANT. Also, the mess halls didn't offer certain foods—like hot roast beef sandwiches, and chicken-in-a-basket—that was popular back in the States. First I decided to put shrimp cocktail on the menu, which became real popular. Then we added chicken-in-a-basket, hamburgers, meat loaf, steak sandwiches, and hot roast beef sandwiches. Sales began to climb. We were doing $40 in food sales when I started, and we ended up grossing $700 a day by the time I left. Rounding out the menu to match the customer made all the difference.

Everything went along fine for the first three months, and then a big problem developed. It was both my first experience in global management and my first real lesson in confrontation as a manager.

We had about fifteen German civilians on our staff, and when Mac left the premises, no one would listen to me. I had the title and the responsibility of "manager-on-duty," but I had no clout. Even today, in most German businesses, you'll rarely find a young person in a position with great authority. In Germany, managers move steadily up the ranks, and the idea of a nineteen-year-old being the boss was something these people could neither understand nor accept. So there was a cultural issue that was already against me.

To make matters worse, under a United Nations pact we weren't supposed to fire any civilians. You had to go through the German government to get them dismissed, and you had to have evidence that they had done something wrong, and that was very complicated to prove. So I had a problem. How do you get people's attention when you don't have the real authority to fire them and they don't accept you as the boss?

I was really upset, but I didn't want to cry to Mac about it. I had never really confronted a big work group like this, but

I felt I had no choice. One night I had had enough, so I called a meeting. Of course, all the Germans could speak or at least understand English, but I brought an interpreter with me just to play it safe.

I told them that Sergeant McCauley had entrusted me with running the Club and I intended to do a good job of it. "I am your boss, and the way you have been treating me is not right," I said. I told them if they did not start accepting me and doing what I said, I would fire each one of them. I said that if they wanted to work for me and do a good job, fine. If not, they could hit the road and never come back.

I was scared as hell that I would be left with no one to work. But I was just as scared that they might stand up and tell me to prove it, and I would have to prove myself up to United Nations specifications, or have an international incident on my hands. I tried not to let my nervousness show and ended with a firmly stated, "Does everyone understand?" as I looked around the room and tried to make eye contact with everyone there. They nodded their heads and not one person left the room. From that day on, I never had a problem. I was in command . . . really in command.

I learned a valuable lesson from that experience. It taught me what authority really meant. If you are given responsibility without authority you cannot do your job. And if you are given authority without people understanding that you have that authority, you can't manage them. Sergeant McCauley always supported me if I deserved it, and if I did something wrong, he wasn't afraid to tell me. He was a disciplinarian, but he was fair and knew how to motivate people. Good management and having someone in charge who cares is the key to any successful operation.

After about a year, things were going so well at the Club that we decided to expand our business. There was a beer garden, run by the military, across the street from us. We ended up taking it over and improving it. Our only competition at the time were "guest houses," local non-military bars that served drinks and some food, and whose main attraction was prostitution. There was a guest house right outside our gate, and there the hookers could come in unescorted. Hookers couldn't come into our places unescorted. They could come if a GI brought them, but they couldn't come through by themselves. That was the right policy, but it also hurt our sales.

I used to give the MPs free sandwiches and food from time to time. It was an investment in community goodwill. Every so often I'd call them up and complain that my business was really slow because I heard there was a lot of prostitution going on at the guest house. I'd tell them, "You ought to go check it out because there could be trouble." The MPs would go in and find something wrong and close them down for two or three hours, and my business would come right back up to where I knew it should be. Of course, I didn't do that all the time, although it was a stand for the right values.

My time working at the Club taught me three more things:

- First, to be successful, your business has to match what your customer wants . . . and, in a restaurant, that means your menu better be right on target.
- Second, the key to a successful confrontation is making sure that people believe you have the authority you say you have.
- Third, it never hurts to have the law on your side, if you know darn well that something fishy is cutting into your business.

I served in Germany for two and a half years but never traveled around to see Europe. I worked every night except Monday, when we were closed, and I really didn't want to do anything else. Besides, I loved what I was doing. It didn't really matter that I hadn't made any real friends and didn't party with the rest of the guys. When I got my discharge papers, I decided that I would return to Fort Wayne and the Hobby House.

4

Colonel-ization

In October of 1953, Sergeant Dave Thomas returned to work at the Hobby House. My first day back was a real special homecoming for me. The whole bunch was there, including Phil Clauss, who met me at the door holding my old apron.

One new waitress caught my eye. Her name was Lorraine Buskirk. She looked quite petite in her blue uniform, but she had a strong voice and a positive attitude—even though she was just eighteen. For the next month or so we kidded back and forth, and eventually, feeling more sure of myself, I started getting a little cocky. I was working as the grillman at the time and I called a lot of the shots. One day we were really busy and I kept pushing the orders out onto the counter at top speed, ringing the bell when an order was ready so the waitresses knew their food was up. Lorraine wasn't picking up her orders fast enough to suit me, so I just stood there ringing the bell over and over. After about ten rings she stormed up to me holding two plates in her hands. "Listen," she said, "would you like me to serve this food or do you want to wear it?"

Who did she think she was talking to me like that? I was an experienced cook and I was in control of the kitchen. That

night we all worked late so I gave Lorraine a lift home, and
I expected her to apologize for what she had said. But nope.
All I got was: "Thanks for the ride. See you tomorrow." I
watched her walk into the house and knew right then that I
liked her. She was different from the other girls. She was
spunky and headstrong. I thought maybe *I'd* apologize to *her*
the next day, but I never did. I just stopped ringing my order
bell so much, which made everybody happy.

Lorraine and I started to date. We didn't have much time
off or a lot of money to spend, but I liked just being with her.
She made me feel special. When we started getting kind of
serious I went to meet her parents. Her stepfather was in the
Air Force and her mother worked at General Electric. They
were really good people and treated me really nice. We talked
a lot about having a family, which is what I wanted more than
anything in the world, so, in 1954, we got married. It was a
small wedding, just the people from work and a few friends of
Lorraine's. We were married in a church in Fort Wayne with
Esther and Lloyd Marquart—Phil's sister and brother-in-
law—standing up for us. None of the waitresses thought it
would last, but thirty-seven years later we're still together and
going strong.

We lived with Lloyd and Esther for a while, and then Phil
loaned me $7,500 to buy a home that Lorraine and I both
liked. Our first daughter, Pam, was born in January 1955. I
left the responsibility of the house and the child to Lorraine.
I had no real idea of what a father should be like. How strict
should he be? Should he spank his kids? How much should he
give in to them? How many things like money and gifts should
be given them? Lorraine made the decisions; I was no model
father who shared in taking care of the home.

The Hobby House was doing a great business because Phil
had an eye for adding new menu items. The highlight of the
menu was still the ten-ounce, paper-thin T-bone, but by now

he had hundreds of other items, and that was both good and
bad. Good—because we had a reputation for variety. Bad—
because it was a devil to manage all that selection and because
the customer didn't see us standing for a particular kind of
food.

Phil was building a new place, too, called the Hobby Ranch
House. Phil had met a guy named Mac McKenny from
Evansville. Mac had a very successful barbecue operation,
Mac's Barbecue, which seated two hundred people and served
ribs, chicken, and potato salad on paper plates with rye bread,
pickles, and onions. That turned Phil on to barbecue as a
possibility for the Hobby Ranch House. In the Army, I had
the sense that barbecue was a coming trend, too.

Phil's six stockholders didn't want us to go into the barbecue business because they didn't think anybody ate barbecue
more than once a week or that many people ate it at all. Phil
and I went to take a look at Mac's Barbecue for ourselves.
They had a really limited menu and I know that carryout
alone the night we were there did $2,000—and this was over
forty years ago. That really made the decision. We went to
Mac and said we wanted to become a franchisee. He said,
"O.K., I'll sell you all your barbecue sauce." We didn't even
pay royalty—a real simple deal compared with franchise ar-
rangements today.

Phil sent me to Evansville for a couple of months to learn
how Mac's operation worked. Mac had a good product and
he approached it a little bit differently from anyone else in the
country. Mac would actually burn the wood and get the coals
sizzling. After the wood stopped burning, the cooks would
throw 100 chickens and 150 pounds of barbecue ribs at a time
into these big pits. It took them two and a half hours to cook
their ribs. When you went to the pits to open them up, you'd
get smoked out.

The name wasn't very strong—Mac's Barbecue was big in

Evansville but not in Fort Wayne—so we called our version the "Hobby Ranch House with Barbecue." Not a short and catchy name for a restaurant, was it? The system was pretty simple. Mac sold us the dry powder, and we added the ketchup, vinegar, and water. We opened up the barbecue place and we started serving ribs on paper plates, with potato salad, baked beans, rye bread, and sliced onion.

The chicken and ribs had a different taste and a better quality than anything we had ever eaten before. That difference set the product apart from whatever else was available. When I returned to Fort Wayne I was named assistant manager and put in charge of the barbecue business at the Hobby Ranch House. Phil put a lot of faith in me and raised my pay to $75.00 a week. I was working twelve- and fourteen-hour days for that salary and was determined to get as much business through those doors as I could. By this time, I was working even harder because Lorraine told me that another child was on the way.

Unfortunately, our barbecue business wasn't going as great as we had hoped. I guess we didn't promote the barbecue as we should have, and we didn't have the name or image for it like Mac's Barbecue. But the main problem was that we didn't stick to Mac's basic program, which was just that—basic. When customers complained about the paper plates we switched to china. But china and silver ran our costs up. When customers said they would prefer rolls to rye bread, we gave them rolls and butter. We later realized that the key to Mac's success was that he picked a limited menu and stuck with it. We had all these other items on our menu—many of which were good—but the variety killed our focus and made the business much harder to manage. That's what did in Howard Johnson's and so many other full-service restaurants: lack of focus and all the complications that came with too much variety.

● ● ●

Phil Clauss continued to be an important part of my life. He was a teacher, a father, and a close friend. He gave me a feeling of security that assured me that if anything happened, I had someone to turn to. Phil was a living textbook, but what made him such an exceptional teacher was that he let me teach him things, too. He gave me the confidence to speak up and even criticize someone much more senior and experienced than I was.

Let me sum it up this way. There was:

Two-Way Teaching in the Phil Clauss Classroom

1. *Phil taught me that I had the skill of "positive criticism."* He would say: "Dave, out of all my employees, you are the one man who combines criticism with good, sound suggestions and recommendations of what to do. That's why I listen to you without flying off the handle." You see, all I did was apply what Frank and George Regas had taught me before.

2. *I taught Phil that he should organize more and be more visible in the restaurant.* I told him he had to start delegating and let us handle more of the load. I told him that the customers needed to see him, too. "When you're so busy working in the back office or the kitchen, doing everybody else's job, you have no time to go up front. And customers like to see the owner. It makes them feel good to have the owner come up to their table and ask if everything is satisfactory. It makes the customer feel important." Phil was aware of this and tried hard, but it was difficult for him to make this work.

3. *Phil taught me to hustle when things seemed slow.* Once Phil hired an efficiency expert from Chicago. This guy

charged us $1,000 and his only advice was to close the restaurant between 2 P.M. and 5 P.M. because we weren't making any money then. That was dumb because if we started breaking shifts and sending home waitresses we'd lose some great people. Instead, Phil called a meeting of the staff and said:

"Let's quit sitting at the table all afternoon smoking cigarettes and talking together.

"Let's be on our feet as soon as a customer comes in.

"Let's be cleaning mirrors and wiping tables.

"Let's be on the move."

We had a bad habit of just sitting around when business was slow. A customer would walk in and we'd wait until he sat down before we got up. Well, we turned our whole business around in the middle of the afternoon with the attitude of looking alive and keeping busy. We got a reputation for *really* being "open for business" in the afternoon when so many restaurants had shut down—mentally if not physically. So much for the efficiency expert.

4. *I taught Phil that you had to promote and keep creating excitement to build the business.* I got him into advertising and thought up new ways to get people talking about the restaurants.

5. *Phil taught me that the world was a school.* He was never satisfied with just standing still and watching the day go by. "Let each day teach you something," he would say. "Go out and look for new ideas."

Phil, his son Dick, and I used to travel around a lot to see what other restaurant operators were doing. He always said that if you can take a trip and come back home with one new idea, you have paid for the trip. And when you come home, always digest what you have seen. Don't get too excited and think that you have to change your entire operation to be like someone else's—you'll be making a big mistake. Take the time to digest your thoughts and only use the new things you have seen that make sense.

I wasn't just a cook anymore. I was a manager and working in all parts of the business. It was great to help Phil's business grow, but I wasn't happy with the amount of money I was making. My son, Kenny, was born in October 1956, and with the responsibility of two kids, I wanted and needed more money. I was still making only $75.00 a week and we were constantly strapped. Somewhere, there had to be a golden egg. When it turned up—and it did—I didn't even recognize it.

As I said, Phil Clauss was always looking to do things better. Most of the time I agreed with him, but the one time I didn't, I was wrong, dead wrong. He had just returned from a National Restaurant Convention at the Palmer House in Chicago and he was raving about a guy he had met, a Kentucky "Colonel," who claimed he had a better way to cook fried chicken.

Phil said that since neither he nor this guy were drinking men, they just kind of bumped into each other in the lobby and talked for three hours while everyone else was out doing the town. He really liked this Harland Sanders. When he described him to me, a sixty-five-year-old with gray hair, goatee, moustache, string tie, and black suit, I raised my eyebrows.

"He's a real character, David. Cusses like a mule skinner but he's invented a recipe and a new way of frying chicken that he guarantees will have customers beating down our doors."

So far the Colonel had sold his "idea" to only a few restaurants in the country, one being Pete Harmon's Dew Drop Inn in Salt Lake City, Utah. He called his product Kentucky

Fried Chicken. The chicken was a menu item for restaurants that did business with the Colonel.

The deal was simple enough. Colonel Sanders would sell you a supply of his secret spices and some Mirromac pressure cookers at $27.50 a piece. And he wanted 5 cents for every chicken you sold. It was strictly a handshake deal. Phil wanted to give it a try, but I didn't. I argued, "Listen, Phil. Why should we pay this guy a nickel a head when we already have good fried chicken ourselves?" A nickel a head could mean $100 a month or more for the Colonel from each restaurant on the program—not bad income back then. I understood why the Colonel wanted to sign us up.

"But we only cook it up on Sundays, Dave," he argued, "because of the amount of work. With his method, we can sell fried chicken every day of the week." Phil had a point. We only messed with chicken on Sunday morning, and then we cooked up at least a hundred head. We fried it in heavy cast-iron skillets, which was a mess and caused grease to splatter all over your arms and face. After frying it, we'd put it in Dutch ovens to cook the meat all the way through. When you considered cleaning and breading, it took about four hours before our chicken was ready to serve.

Colonel Sanders claimed his chicken only took thirty minutes because he fried and steamed it in one step. He also claimed it was "a damned sight better" than any chicken anywhere in the United States. And it was exotic. People in Indiana were curious about chicken that had a "Kentucky" put in front of it. People wanted to try something that they thought was different. I'm sure Kentucky Fried Chicken meant a whole lot more outside of Kentucky than inside it. It's still the same today. Isn't it funny how often Maine lobster is served on Florida menus? Why do restaurants outside of New York feature New York strip steaks and restaurants in New York feature Kansas City strip steaks?

About two months later, I met the Colonel himself. Phil didn't tell me he was coming to the restaurant where I worked as an assistant manager. I guess Phil wanted to surprise me, but when the front door swung open, who else could it have been? I had never seen a black suit like that in my life. (The Colonel's "white suit" period started later.) The coat had long tails and fit him perfectly. His graying goatee was perfectly trimmed and he carried a gold-tipped cane. Colonel Sanders was one of a kind.

He sat down in a corner booth all by himself and ordered a plate of ribs. (Yep, he licked his fingers.) When he was finished, he paid his check and asked to see the manager (meaning me). He introduced himself and asked if I knew him. I pretended I didn't even though I knew all about him. We sat down over a cup of coffee, and he talked to me like an old friend. I've never met a better salesman. When he left, I had a sense this man was going to change my life.

When I finally tasted Kentucky Fried Chicken in a restaurant in Michigan City, Indiana, I knew it was a really good product. I had to tell Phil Clauss that I was wrong, something I didn't like to do very often. We tried the chicken at another restaurant, and we had the same great result. I really liked the gravy. It was made with heated milk that was blended into shortening, flour, and chicken cracklings. The result was thick, creamy milk gravy.

Maybe this Colonel in a white Cadillac had something. Even though I was to make a lot of money in chicken, the funniest thing was that I personally hated chicken.

The chicken and dumplings I saw as a nine-year-old at Salstrum's restaurant looked great, but my taste for chicken went bad when I was about fourteen. My dad was a superintendent at a bus company in Tennessee at the time. One of his workers who lived in the mountains invited us over for dinner one Sunday afternoon. I'll never forget the house: It had no paint, the porch was half burned down, and there weren't any screens or curtains on the windows. When we sat down to eat, some chickens started walking through the house. When they passed by my chair, the smell and the flies they drew turned my stomach. I couldn't stand it and had to go to the car. That was it. The end of me and chicken.

In the mid-fifties, we were given our first franchise from Colonel Harland Sanders. It took about three months to put Kentucky Fried Chicken into both of Phil's restaurants. We had to modify our stoves to fit the Colonel's special pots, and he wanted to be sure we knew how to "do his chicken right." You couldn't believe how particular he was about his crackling gravy. Cracklings are bits of fried flour that flake off the chicken after it's cooked, and you had to add enough cracklings to the gravy or the Colonel would really get after you.

When we started selling Kentucky Fried Chicken at the Ranch House, our business really took off. Customers would come in, order chicken at the cash register, and then stand and wait while somebody went to the back to get it. We had people lined up out the door.

Kentucky Fried Chicken was a sensation from day one; but why? We knew it tasted good, but there had to be more to it. We did some customer surveys (which were nearly unknown in the restaurant business back then) and found out that people liked the idea of taking food home to eat. It was convenient and saved a lot of time. Also, people were traveling more. They said they were going to the lake or the park, and the wife (O.K., today it's the spouse) was home making salads, so with our chicken, their picnic fixings were complete.

In those days people didn't buy food to take home except for an occasional bag of hamburgers, so we were on the edge of a new phenomenon and we were smart enough to see it. Chicken was halfheartedly sold through drive-in restaurants, but it was usually tough and almost always greasy. Phil and

I knew we had a superior product and thought the time was right to specialize in take-home chicken by opening a room strictly for carryout.

Within a few months, we built one of the first places in the United States totally devoted to carryout or take-home chicken. With this room, we helped pioneer the idea of carry-out. Before long, we were taking in $3,000–$4,000 every Sunday, which was our biggest day for chicken. At one point someone told us we were one of the largest places for carryout chicken in the whole U.S.

Kentucky Fried Marketing

1. *Kentucky Fried Chicken was a turning point in restaurant marketing.* Promoting and advertising Kentucky Fried Chicken was another idea Phil and I pioneered. The Colonel was feeling his way into franchising and no one knew much about it. He sold strictly by word of mouth. He was a great salesman, but he was his only salesman. The company consisted of the Colonel and his wife. The Colonel was sixty-five and his goal was to make $1,000 a month. That was better than his Social Security check, and he said it would keep him and his wife real good. "We'll be able to travel around the country and have fun doing it and help people at the same time," he explained to me.

Phil and I were more ambitious than that and knew we could sell more chicken. We were impatient and didn't want to wait for one neighbor to tell another about us, so we started promoting. In those days you just opened up and cooked the best food you could and hoped for word of mouth to spread your name. Image was a new word, franchise was a new word, promotion, marketing and merchandising were all new words in the restaurant business.

2. *This snowballing idea of takeout food made packaging real important.* Few people know this, but selling chicken in a bucket was really Phil's idea. When the Colonel first started coming around with his pots, herbs, and spices in the backseat of his Cadillac, the only packaging idea he had was the dinner box, which was a simple cardboard rectangle. It showed three baby chicks on one side, "My Old Kentucky Home" on the other, and held three pieces of chicken, mashed potatoes, gravy, coleslaw, rolls, and honey all for $1.10. But Phil and I saw the possibilities way beyond the box. It wasn't big enough for large families who wanted a lot of chicken or for parties. Plus, a stack of boxes was hard to carry.

Phil was riding on a train to Portland, Oregon, and he couldn't sleep. He went into the smoker with a pencil and paper and doodled up this idea of creating a bucket for chicken. He decided on how many pieces should go into it along with biscuits, honey, and gravy. He set a price of $3.50 without even knowing what the cost was. When Phil returned to Fort Wayne, he found some buckets similar to what we got ten pounds of cottage cheese in. They were red-and-white striped and paraffin-coated on the outside. The only problem was, as we discovered the hard way, they were not designed to hold hot food.

About a week after we introduced the bucket, a lady came in wearing a fur coat—and the wax that had melted all over her coat. Another person had a new Chrysler with plaid cloth seat covers. He set the bucket on the backseat and the wax got all over his upholstery. We settled these complaints, thanks to a local dry cleaner, but knew we had to make some design changes.

We changed the coatings on the bucket, found a manufacturer, and asked Phil's brother-in-law, Jim Chamberlain, who ran an advertising agency in Fort Wayne, to do some sketches of the Colonel for us to put on the bucket. The Colonel had no money at the time, so he offered Jim a penny-per-bucket royalty for his work. Being a struggling artist, Jim said he wanted a flat $10,000. Tough as it was, the Colonel came up with the money, but Jim kicked himself for years for not taking the royalty deal!

3. *People liked a person backing up their takeout food.* People may giggle about the Colonel's shoe-string tie, his gold-tipped cane, and his white goatee, or his white Cadillac, but they created an image. (I later learned the Colonel first had his beard bleached white. First, his barber tried to do it with Clorox, and it turned orange. Then he went to a beauty shop and had the job done right. Later, natural aging took care of the problem altogether.)[3] Food is a personal thing, and it's tied closely to family life. People want to know the values of the person who is ladling out the goods. Harland Sanders stood for values that people understood and liked. It was just the next step from what had already happened with packaged goods. Remember, people thought of Betty Crocker and Uncle Ben as real people behind the products, too.

4. *Because the Colonel was such a personality, we were able to get him on local TV and radio shows, which led to plenty of free publicity.* He really attracted attention in his famous double-breasted white suit with black string tie. It could be the middle of winter, and there'd be this guy in a white suit and goatee, a likable grandfather-type, a master showman, talking about his "secret" recipe of eleven herbs and spices for cooking chicken, America's hospitality dish. Everybody wants in on a secret, so people listened. He'd get all riled up about the difference between bad fried chicken and good fried chicken, so you'd think it was a federal case.

[3]John Ed Pearce, *The Colonel* (New York: Doubleday & Co., 1982).

If we promised to bring a bucket or two of chicken along, we could get him on plenty of shows. Sometimes, we could trade them for an outright ad. This was back before the "payola" stink, so maybe it was "chicken-ola," I don't know. When he was on the radio, sometimes I used to nudge him to keep him awake. I was always worried he'd go to sleep. I used to think, I'm sure glad he's doing those interviews and not me! And today I'm doing the same thing that he was doing.

If you've got an angle, you can get plenty of publicity. When billboard signs go up in baseball and football stadiums, the thousands of people in the stands aren't the real audience—but the millions of people at home watching their televisions are. A committed Christian figured this out, and some of you may remember this: He would go to pro football games and hold up a sign that said "John 3:16" in the end zone when a field goal or extra point was kicked. What does "John 3:16" have to say? I'm not telling. The point of holding up the sign was getting people to open up their Bibles, and I bet plenty of people did just that.

Traveling with the Colonel was a caution. During one of the early trips we made together in the fifties, we drove to Houston, Texas, where he wanted to stay at a $15-a-day hotel. This was a lot of money in those days! I was too ashamed to admit that I didn't have that kind of cash, and Lorraine had to wire me some money. As if that wasn't bad enough, on that same trip, the Colonel let me use his famous white Cadillac and I blundered onto a tar road and got it all speckled up. It took me hours of hand rubbing to get all the tar off, but I made sure it was perfect when I took it back to him or he would have cussed me out for days.

Harland Sanders's temper was legend. After ordering a bicarbonate of soda in a restaurant he got the owner so riled up in a spat over the price of the tonic that the owner threw a heavy sugar shaker at the Colonel. The owner succeeded in breaking the glass door to his own restaurant! Another time, the Colonel got into a fight in a parking lot after an exchange of insults and hurt his opponent's leg with a chunk of concrete.[4]

Other times the Colonel could surprise you and do just the opposite of what you'd expect. Once, he went to New York to sell a franchise and the potential franchisee took him around Manhattan in a limousine. The franchisee asked the Colonel, "Where should we drop you off?" They were thinking he'd say the Waldorf-Astoria or the Plaza. Instead, he said, "Just drop me off at my Association." "Where would that be, sir?" the chauffeur asked. "At the YMCA," the Colonel said.

Another time, we were driving through Hammond, Indiana, during a snowstorm. I was a smoker then, but I didn't know that he hated smoking. He never told me. The roads were like glass. Suddenly, he made me pull the car to the side of the road, yanked the ashtray from the dashboard, and actually threw it out the window. "I hate smoking," he fumed. "It makes me sick and I won't tolerate it!" I didn't smoke the rest of the trip, but it would have been a lot easier if he just had said something first.

The Colonel had a real personal style with the way he ran things. I should know—I worked with him for thirteen years. Although I disagreed with some of what he did and preached, I still use much of his philosophy today at Wendy's.

---

[4] John Ed Pearce, *The Colonel.*

The Colonel's Recipe for
Down-Home Management

1. *No good business will go anywhere without high standards.*
The Colonel was a perfectionist when it came to fixing his
chicken. I admired him for sticking to his guns. He didn't
have much money in those days and he wanted his business
to grow, but he wasn't so hungry that he'd let the quality of
his product slide.

When the Colonel gave us a franchise, he didn't just ride off
into the sunset. He'd come back to check on us every three
weeks or so. I can still hear his badgering today: "We want
customers, don't we?" "We want sales, don't we?" "And we
want to uphold the Colonel's standards of quality, don't we?"
He made business standards a personal affair. He was right.

2. *Cleanliness is the single most important ingredient on a
restaurant's menu.* What really gave fast-food chains a boost
is that they were reliably clean. Too many people were nervous about the "greasy spoon" diners that populated the
American landscape. Ptomaine and food poisoning really
seemed to happen more often back then because many restaurants didn't have the clear rules and guidelines on storing and
cooking food that they do today. Colonel Sanders was a real
stickler for cleanliness, and every Wendy's restaurant today
aims to be the same.

3. *You can criticize people and still leave them feeling finger-
lickin' good.* The Colonel was a really nice man but he had a
hot temper. If something wasn't right, he'd let loose with a
string of cuss words that could make you feel two feet high.
He didn't want to cuss. In fact, he felt really bad about it. He
was a religious man and he prayed to stop cussing, but he was
"just attached to it," as he would say, all bewildered.

I liked his philosophy but didn't agree with his style. From the Colonel I learned to set down firm rules and guidelines, but I also learned that tantrums weren't the best way to solve a problem. But, then, Lorraine had already taught me that lesson when she put a damper on my bell ringing.

The Colonel used to tell me, "Dave, you have to be direct with people. Tell 'em off when they need it, but leave them feeling good. If you're kind to them at the end of the talk, they won't remember all the yelling that came before." But the Colonel was wrong about this, because people do remember all the yelling that came before. They resent it, and it weakens their motivation. So I remember his message, but I use it with a very different style than he did.

There were times when you might not have agreed with the Colonel, but you couldn't help liking him. His objective was really to help people do well so they could buy homes, send their kids to college, and go on vacations. He especially liked to see older people go into business so they could retire and have an income.

The Colonel had his problems, though, because he wasn't a very good businessman. He had some money troubles, and he wouldn't always deliver on his promises. He wasn't trying to cheat anybody; he just worked too hard, overbooked himself, and would forget what he told you. The older he got, the more tired and cynical he became. Still, his integrity stayed strong even though he became more irritable and harder to work with. Kentucky Fried Chicken was his last shot and he was determined to make it a success.

Phil really helped the Colonel expand. He often sent people who were considering buying a franchise to see our operation. He didn't have the time or people to talk to everyone, and he thought we were really good salesmen. That really added to my contacts in the restaurant industry, and that helped later when I was franchising Wendy's.

Working closely with the Colonel over those years made me

think about retirement and being a senior citizen for the first real time in my life. I'm not quite sixty, so maybe I shouldn't talk; but I've watched plenty of people who are sixty plus, and I have three conclusions that I've come to.

Dave's Advice to Seniors

- *Don't retire . . . age is just a number.* I'm really against seniors retiring. We have seniors working in our restaurants. The eighteen-to-twenty-five-year-old group is the most rapidly shrinking part of the population. That's the age group from which we used to get all our staff. We have people in our restaurants who are eighty years old! They're fantastic. They enjoy it. They know all the customers. People who have always been busy probably *need* to be busy doing something. One senior told me a few days ago, "You have to have a reason to put your makeup on in the morning and get out of the house."

- *Do what you want.* When I say don't retire, that doesn't mean that seniors shouldn't change jobs. More than anything, it's important that senior citizens be in something they really like to do. Some folks join the Peace Corps. Others do community service. Still others go into business on their own. Stay active, but stay active doing what YOU want to do.

- *Take a walk on the wild side.* Colonel Sanders dressed up like he walked off the set of *Gone With the Wind*. Clara "Where's-the-Beef?" Peller used to give press conferences, even though she couldn't hear the reporters' questions. Grandma Minnie Sinclair would use five or six testers in the perfume department to blend her own personal fragrance on the Saturday trips to the five-and-dime. All the fun seniors I have ever met were a little eccentric. Wait till my kids see what I've got planned for myself when I turn sixty-five!

People are living longer these days. Plenty of people spend twenty to twenty-five years being a "senior citizen." The way I look at it, why not figure out how to do it right, right off the bat, when there are just sixty candles on the cake?

5

The Little Guy's Guide to Success

Kentucky Fried Chicken made it possible for me to meet
Kenny King, back in the late fifties at the Hobby Ranch
House. He and a couple of his people came to Fort Wayne to
see what Kentucky Fried Chicken was all about. Kenny became my role model for success. He died in 1972, but I hold
his memory dear.

Kenny King owned about twenty restaurants in Cleveland,
Ohio, most of which were drive-ins. His name and face were
familiar to me because he was written up in the industry
magazines all the time. I was impressed with Kenny King the
moment I laid eyes on him. He pulled up to our restaurant in
a brand-new Cadillac. He was wearing a finely tailored suit
and a white shirt that didn't show a wrinkle. He was somewhere in his fifties, and I guess you could sum it up by saying
that Kenny was a class act all the way.

At first, Kenny said he really wasn't interested in the
chicken business. He saw himself as a hamburger man, who
believed in coffee shops and drive-ins. Then he ordered a
chicken dinner and asked me to sit down with him. He began
asking all kinds of questions about the Colonel and KFC. I

was only the assistant manager of one restaurant in Fort Wayne, and yet he put me on an equal footing with himself. He listened and told me he was impressed with how much I knew about the restaurant business. I told him why I was sold on Kentucky Fried Chicken, and when he tried it, I think he was convinced himself.

Kenny invited me to Cleveland to see his operation. I was completely impressed by his suite of offices in the Williamson Building. He started off by showing me his profit-and-loss statement. Here I was, twenty-five years old, making less than $100 a week, talking like an equal to someone who was making over $100,000 a year.

Today, too many MBAs make a lot of money BEFORE they're thirty, and all they know about business is how to read profit-and-loss statements. And I'm not real sure how well some of these MBAs do reading P&Ls. One time, I was invited up to Cambridge to speak at the Harvard Business School. During the question period, two students in the audience argued with me that Wendy's was making extra money on our chili because we had already accounted for the meat as a hamburger patty that was cooked too long to be served as a hamburger. At first, I thought they might be funning me. After a while, it was clear they were serious. I had to explain that we still "owned" each patty until we sold it to the customer as either chili or a sandwich. If it was chili, then the meat cost was just a part of chili. That was one scary experience. It's the only time I've ever thought that dropping out of high school might NOT have been a mistake.

Back then, the fact that Kenny King made more than a $100,000 a year really turned my head. When Kenny pointed to the coffee table in front of us and said it cost $300, he did that to make a point. He told me, "Hey, son, this is America. If I can do it so can you. All you've got to do is work hard and have ethics. You've got to have a philosophy." Kenny also said he was one drink away from being a drunk. When I tried to compliment him for that once, he said, "Hey, we're supposed to be sober, aren't we?" He belonged to Alcoholics Anonymous and hadn't had a drink in thirty years because he had a philosophy of life: Follow the Ten Commandments. "In the morning you've got to get up and look in the mirror. You've got to be honest with the guy in the mirror before anyone else. The support of your family is the most important thing that you have in your life." The Ten Commandments, being honest with himself first, and supporting his family were the keys to Kenny's philosophy.

That night Kenny took me to dinner at the Cleveland Athletic Club—the first private club I'd ever been to—and he tipped the waiter $15. He told me, "I've got the money, I've got the responsibility to share it." I decided right then and there that I wanted to be like Kenny King. I would work even harder, buy nice things for myself and my family, join a country club, help other people, and never forget the Man Upstairs who made it all possible. Kenny knew he was swaying me, but he cautioned me, too. "It's good you're impressed with all this," he said, "but don't take yourself too seriously, and remember, you don't have all the answers."

In the end, Kenny got together with the Colonel and made a fortune on Kentucky Fried Chicken. Kenny never forgot me, and I made him the role model I really wanted to be like. We never talked about it this way, but I just picked him out as my mentor and crawled under his wing. Although Kenny was successful, he was no big celebrity executive. Many people want to link up with superstars. The way I see it, sometimes you can learn more from a common, everyday person who cares about others and who has achieved something than some guy with a big ego who just wants a bunch of followers.

In 1959 the Colonel sent a real estate man from Columbus,

Ohio, to see Phil at the Ranch House. This guy and a friend of his wanted to open up some KFC franchises in Columbus. They wanted Phil to invest with them as an equal partner. Phil agreed on the condition that I would act as their "operations advisor." These weren't restaurant people, but with me advising and checking on their operation, Phil felt comfortable and was willing to take the risk.

I stayed in Fort Wayne but went to Columbus once a month to meet with the new franchisees. They quickly opened up one Hobby Ranch House Take-Home after another. Their quality was slipshod, their customer service was poor, they had weak managers, and they were late paying their bills. While I was supposed to be their advisor, they didn't take any of my advice, starting from day one when they picked their sites. They had four restaurants in operation in 1960, and by 1961 they were in deep trouble. Phil was nervous that he would lose his investment because the Colonel was ready to pull the Columbus franchises. He asked me to go to Columbus and take over the four failing stores.

I was excited about the chance. I wasn't making as much money as I wanted at the Ranch House. With the addition of my daughter, Molly Jo, in 1958, and Melinda Lou, in June of 1961, my family responsibilities were growing rapidly. I wanted to give it some more thought, but I knew what my answer would be.

Except for Phil, who had a stake in the deal, all my mentors were against my going to Columbus. Kenny King warned, "Just know what you're getting into, Dave. It could be a big mistake. You want to push this carryout thing, but I think you need a coffee-shop type of operation. You're a smart young man, though, and I'll help you any way I can."

The Colonel exploded when he heard about it. "You're stupid if you go there," he said. "I thought you were smarter than that. That operation is on its ass and you're going to uproot your wife and kids and make a G.D. fool of yourself. Wise up, boy. You'll paint yourself right into a corner. It's a one-way street going nowhere."

Well, I was going nowhere at the Ranch House, too. No matter how much money we made I probably wouldn't see much more than I was seeing. I had the title of vice president, but I still wore an apron every day, and I still worked the grill every day, and I still earned $27 a day before taxes.

As to business, I think people make it too complicated. When I was eight years old I knew I wanted to be in the restaurant business, and I was now given the chance to accomplish that goal. Positive thinking and a burning desire were the most important things I had going for me. And then Phil made me a fair and honest deal, which was the final ingredient in my plan.

Phil bought back all the outstanding stock for 50 cents on the dollar from the two guys in Columbus who had the franchise. The total debt in the company was $250,000, which Phil assumed in full. Phil would raise my salary from $115 to $135 a week, give me a nickel commission on each chicken I sold, plus 15% of the profits every month after paying the first $500 to the company. He also told me I could buy stock in the company. "You pay me back the $250,000 I have in this thing and I will sell you 40% of the company (which was the Columbus franchise for Kentucky Fried Chicken) for $65," he said. "I know it's a long shot, Dave, but I think you can do it."

Phil's offer was everything I had been waiting for. I have said that when the time is right to make a move, a person just knows it. Deep down the green light clicks on. I knew I was ready. Lorraine and I talked it through, and we figured we could handle the downside. After all, at that time, we didn't have all that much to lose.

Lorraine told me to do whatever I thought best. She would have to give up friends and family to move to Columbus, and she would still be raising the kids almost by herself, but she knew I wanted to get somewhere fast, and she supported me.

My clearest memory of this time was how Lorraine was such a great support for me, and such a model parent. As a parent, I really didn't have any role models. Lorraine came from a really strong family. As a result, she knew what to do, and she did it: Girl Scouts and paper drives, homework and teacher conferences. Lorraine did a fantastic job, but I have to confess that I cheated my kids by not being involved enough in raising them. You see, I didn't give them a very good idea of what a father should be like so that when they raised their own children they didn't have a model to look back on. Despite this, my four married kids do pretty well splitting up the job of raising children (so far, we have nine grandchildren) between husband and wife. So, Lorraine—again—may have succeeded in doing the work for both of us.

In January 1962, with a net worth of $3,000 and forty bucks in my pocket, I went to Columbus. With a new baby, I didn't feel the time was right to move my family, so I stayed in a motel for two weeks and then found a sleeping room that was much cheaper. I traveled back and forth to Fort Wayne, but after a few months the loneliness got to me and I found I really missed my wife and kids. So, we decided to buy a house in Columbus. Since I was working fourteen hours a day we set up an appointment at eleven o'clock one night to see some houses. The only one that I could afford was in the suburb of Westerville. We assumed a G.I. loan for $98 a month including taxes and insurance, with a down payment of $3,000. I called Lorraine and said, "We got a house!" In June, with the help of a U-Haul trailer and a flat bed truck, I moved my family to Columbus.

With my family now settled, I could give 100% of my attention to bringing back the KFC business, and I did.

In February 1962 we were doing about $2,500 a week in all

four KFC stores. The first thing I did was to size up the managers. Each one of them was in over his head, and I had no choice but to let each of them go.

There wasn't much money for the day-to-day operations, but the second thing I did was to go in and paint everything. The stores needed a fresh, new, clean look, and I remembered what an impact painting the mess halls had made in Frankfurt. Sprucing the places up, I figured, would be good for the employees as well as the customers.

Sales were dismal, our credit was zero, and even the Colonel insisted on making his deliveries C.O.D. And the Colonel didn't spare me any advice when he saw me. "I'm telling you for the last time, Dave," he said. "As your friend, get out now while you can. Things are just too far gone here. Listen to the Colonel, boy." I thanked him, paid him, and told him, "It'll turn around. It will. You'll see, in a few months, it'll turn."

Every day, I wanted to know how much money I was making, so I devised a daily report sheet that my office manager had ready for me every morning. I didn't really know anything about bookkeeping, but these were the numbers I needed to know. On this form were daily sales, labor costs, food costs, and how much cash we had in the bank on a day-by-day basis. The third thing I did, then, was to focus on the key numbers for the business. Later, the Colonel liked the form so much, he started to use it throughout Kentucky Fried Chicken.

The fourth thing that we did was to promote. Advertising and promoting had always brought in a lot of new customers at the Fort Wayne Ranch House, so even though I didn't have any money I knew I was good at making deals. The local radio station manager knew I couldn't afford to buy ads, but he swapped me radio spots for some chicken. His deal set me thinking.

That chicken swap at the radio station led to the biggest

breakthrough of all: We had to focus these four takeout places in a way that made sense to the customers. It dawned on me that it wasn't our menu that was drawing people in. It was our chicken! I drove straight to our closest restaurant and grabbed one of the menus. It was too full, too crowded—that was my problem. Within a few weeks, the menu was slimmed down to chicken, salads, dessert, and beverages. Since nobody had ever heard the name Hobby Ranch House, I changed the name of our restaurants to Colonel Sanders Kentucky Fried Chicken Take-Home.

Once we had the focus on chicken, we promoted that focus even more. I started running price specials every day of the week. A regular dinner of three pieces of chicken, mashed potatoes, gravy, and a roll sold for $1.25. With a coupon, it went for 79 cents. The houses surrounding the restaurants were swimming in coupons. Business picked up almost right away, and any money I had leftover I plowed into advertising.

The sixth thing we did was to identify ourselves in a way that the customer wouldn't forget. I met with a guy named Terry Dorgan at a sign company and told him that I wanted a sign that looked like a wobbling bucket. Dorgan looked at me like I was crazy.

"Wobble?" he asked.

"Yes," I said. "I want you to take this bucket and somehow get lights under it so it glows and stands out so people on the freeway can see it. I also want it to wobble."

"Wobble?" he asked again.

"Look," I said, starting to lose my temper. "Wobble! Wobble! I want it to move round and round."

"Oh, rotate!" he said, relieved that he had finally gotten my meaning. "You want the bucket to revolve. I see." It took him about two weeks to come up with my illuminated, revolving bucket, and he did a fantastic job. That's how the bucket sign got started, and the Colonel began using my "wobbling" bucket in all of his stores. That bucket sign came to stand for Kentucky Fried Chicken, the same way that three balls over the door meant you were a pawnbroker, or a whirling candy-cane lamp meant you were a barber.

As KFC got bigger and bigger, the Colonel started to lose control. He insisted on calling all the shots, but more and more franchisees stopped listening. It was no longer a big happy family where the Colonel knew everyone on a first name basis.

In the mid-sixties, the Colonel sold the business to John Y. Brown, Jr., and Jack Massey. Brown later went on to become governor of Kentucky and to marry the 1971 Miss America, Phyllis George. Jack Massey went on to found Hospital Corporation of America and Volunteer Capital. Jack was a charmer—six feet tall, with a shock of white hair, and always dressed in a perfectly pressed blue shirt. He was probably Nashville's best-kept secret. A man of very high integrity, he had started out from simple beginnings. I think he learned to deal with people so well from his first trade as a pharmacist. Later, Jack was a valued advisor to me in the development and expansion of Wendy's, and he even became a Wendy's franchisee himself.

John Brown and Jack Massey offered Colonel Sanders $2 million with $500,000 down and a note to cover the rest. He would receive a salary of $40,000 a year for as long as he lived, and he would receive residuals for TV commercials and promotional appearances, but he got no stock. Massey and Brown took the business public. I have always been lucky when it comes to timing because right before they went public, I borrowed the money to buy $10,000 worth of KFC stock. Later it was worth plenty.

The Colonel called me late one night and in a trembling voice told me he had decided to sell out. "What do you think, Dave? Did I do the right thing?" I told him that since the deal was done, he shouldn't worry, and he and his wife should enjoy themselves on the money he earned. Down deep, I knew that he had been too active a person to be happily retired. The Colonel never could live with his selling of KFC. As long as I knew him, he cursed himself for what he called the biggest mistake of his life. Five years later John Y. Brown and Jack Massey turned around and sold KFC for $130 million.

For me, things were going gangbusters. My daughter, Lori, was born in March 1967. I paid Phil back the $250,000 debt and received 40% of the company, and I was opening my fifth store. It was about then that I had a falling out with the Colonel. Even though he had sold out his interest in KFC, he was still a spokesman for the company, and he still saw the business as HIS concept. He was afraid that the big boys who bought him out and who "didn't know a drumstick from a pig's ear" would ruin it. Even things that didn't make a difference set the Colonel off. The new management had come up with a simpler way to drain grease off the chicken by just dumping it onto wire racks. It was less time-consuming and a lot easier than the Colonel's way, which was to ladle the grease off by hand. The Colonel hated the new "dump" system because he said it bruised the chicken.

As I was getting set for the grand opening of my fifth store, I got a frantic call from the Colonel. "I hear you're using that new system to drain my chicken," he said in an angry voice. I explained how it saved time and affected neither the look nor the taste.

"Let me tell you something, boy," the Colonel declared. "If you dump my chicken you are slapping the Colonel right in the face." I tried to reason with him, but he said he'd never talk to me again. We saw each other maybe once or twice after that before he died at the age of ninety, but the relationship was history. To this day, I really admire him and like him, even though he was a tough customer to get along with sometimes. When I had the KFC restaurants, I even took to wearing black string ties, just like he did, until people started asking me what band I played with!

Steadily, over six years, the business grew and grew. Kentucky Fried Chicken was in the market to buy back some of its more successful stores from franchisees. In 1968 Phil Clauss and I decided the time was right for us to sell our stores to the company. We sold our stock in the franchise for approximately $1.7 million in KFC stock.

Based on my deal with Phil, my share was 40%. In addition, the $10,000 worth of stock I'd bought turned out to be worth about $1 million on paper. Here I was at age thirty-five with a net worth of $1 million! Knowing I had the money was a great feeling, but more important, I proved to myself that I was able to do about anything I wanted to do. It was a big security thing. I didn't have to worry about starving the next week, and the money in the bank took the sting out of what my dad had said about my not being able to hold a job.

The turnaround of Kentucky Fried Chicken in Columbus was the big breakthrough for me. It made everything else possible in my career. When I look back at how it was achieved, I see there were six simple steps. Many business turnarounds are much more complicated, but these six steps are probably a part of even the most complex, big-scale turnarounds you'll ever hear about.

Dave's Six Steps for
Bringing Back a Dying Business

1. *Get rid of the dead wood in management.* For me, this was an easy step to take. I knew the business much better than any of the people we replaced in Columbus. Sometimes, it's just best to clear away the managers so that you can see the

problems for what they are. But, I should add, if you have to let people go these days, make sure you run everything by your lawyer first.

2. *Paint the place.* Some managers clean house with a broom. I do it with a paint brush. Any business that's on its back is bound to have low morale. You have to let your employees and your customers know that you have confidence and that you intend to be around. You don't always have to do this with a paint brush. Maybe it's a new letterhead or a new couch in the reception room if you run an office business.

3. *Get on top of the basic numbers.* With personal computers today, this is actually harder, not easier. You can drown in data in even the simplest business these days. The trick is to get the four or five measures that really make a difference and to concentrate on them every day or at least every week. That's what our daily report was meant to do.

4. *Promote.* Even before you have the business figured out, you can usually promote and advertise your best items—the ones with the best appeal and a good profit margin. You may have to lean on these real hard until you have your direction planned out.

5. *Figure out the business and focus it.* The key in my case was deciding to be in the chicken business in Columbus and to get rid of the pork chops and other items. Today, they call that carving out a "niche" in the market.

6. *Identify yourself so the customer won't forget you.* In my case, the wobbling bucket sign did the trick. The key is to pick an attention-getting symbol or sign AFTER you focus your business, not before. And it has to mean something to people. It has to build an image.

How did Lorraine and I celebrate becoming millionaires? We took ourselves out to dinner, and it wasn't fried chicken, either! Lorraine has never been one to spend money foolishly, so I didn't have to remind her that we were just wealthy on paper. She did splurge on one thing, though. She had a swimming pool built for the kids in the backyard. It was in the shape of a chicken!

Lorraine deserves plenty of the credit for our getting as far as we did. Today, it's very common for both husband and wife to work. I was lucky to have Lorraine at home full-time to raise the family and look after personal business. From what I've seen, when both parents work, at times one of them may feel more pressure or strain than the other. That means the other partner has to play more of a support role. Based on what Lorraine did for me, here are some ways I think couples can be a real help to each other in demanding times.

Supporting Your Spouse

1. *Guard your spouse's "free" time.* When I managed the KFC stores to a turnaround, the only time I carved out for myself was to sleep late on Saturday mornings. To keep the kids quiet so I could doze longer, Lorraine would organize games for them to play, create chores, or send them outside. She devised ways to protect my free time.

2. *Share authority.* When I would be eating dinner with the family on weekends and the kids would ask Lorraine for money or permission to go places (like the movies) or do things (like bike rides) I used to get angry. Then I realized I wasn't there much of the time, and they just naturally asked Mom for things. A spouse can be a big help in taking the lead in parental decision-making, but both must share the author-

ity. Lorraine was really making things easier for me, but I was kind of slow and it took me a while to catch on.

3. *Think flexibility.* When Lorraine thought about dinner for me, she automatically thought about a dinner that could be reheated because she had no sure idea when I'd be coming home from work. A saying in our family used to be, "Just because dinner is cooked doesn't mean it will be eaten."

4. *Keep an eye on the calendar.* I hate to confess how many birthdays would have been forgotten and how many holidays would have been ruined if Lorraine hadn't done the planning and kept the dates in mind.

5. *Timing is everything.* Among spouses, saying the right thing at the right time can really help a marriage. Knowing when to speak up and when to remain silent is equally important. At certain times, there are no truer words than "Silence is Golden."

Just after Phil and I sold out to the parent company, Jack Massey and John Brown offered me a job as regional head of operations for all the KFC stores east of the Mississippi, from Miami to Michigan. That was about three hundred stores. The job paid a $50,000-a-year salary, and I took it. I still had it in my head to open my own restaurant, and I was more convinced than ever that it would be a place selling hamburgers, but I wasn't ready to make the move yet. I saw what McDonald's was doing, and I knew I could do better. Still, I needed the security of a regular salary a little bit longer and the KFC job seemed like the right thing to do.

One of the first things I did in my new position at KFC was to hire a controller for my region. I wasn't good at accounting and I knew I needed a "numbers" man. I had heard about a guy named Ron Musick, who worked for the Ernst and Ernst accounting firm (now Ernst and Young) in Nashville. I was supposed to interview Ron when he came up to meet me, but I got tied up in a meeting. He'd been waiting a long time in the lobby to see me. When we had a break I poked my head out and asked, "Do you want the job?" He said, "I suppose so." And that was the beginning of a terrific relationship that goes on today with Ron as a senior vice president of Wendy's. But, Ron still won't let me forget that first meeting. "You could have at least said, hello, how are you!" is something I still hear from him.

I was traveling five days a week in my new job, and I really missed my family. I tried to troubleshoot the operations, but KFC was really getting "corporate," with a lot of Mickey Mouse memos. After a few more months, I asked to be transferred to acquisitions. It didn't involve so much traveling, and when I did have to travel, it would be aboard KFC's private jet. My job was to find new franchisees and help acquire stores. I reported straight to John Brown, who just left me alone to do my own thing. No memos . . . but no motivation, either.

In the meantime I invested $50,000 in another firm called National Diversified, which was in a different kind of restaurant business that didn't compete with Kentucky Fried Chicken. I introduced the head of National Diversified to Brown, who hired him to build five or six stores for them in Tulsa. And then one day, John Brown called me into his office. "Dave," he said, "we've got a problem, and it might involve a conflict of interest. We know that you have a significant block of stock in National Diversified, and since they've signed a deal with KFC it may present a conflict of interest."

He told me the best way to relieve this problem was for me to sell my stock in National Diversified to KFC for what I paid for it. I knew by then my stock would have a market value of about $2 million if I could have found someone to buy it, but I didn't want to be involved in a conflict of interest.

I never questioned John Brown because I trusted him. He told me I did something I shouldn't have done, and like a big dummy, I believed him. I sold my stock to KFC, trusting John Brown, and thinking that I was doing the right thing. A friend later told me that was a wrong move. There was no conflict of interest. Since I was not a corporate officer of KFC and never made any major decisions or signed any deals for them, I was just an employee.

I decided to go to the Board of KFC and ask for my stock back. They said "no" right away and wouldn't even listen to my side. As to my work, John Brown went out of his way to compliment me on the job I was doing. In fact, I felt like I was getting very little done in the job, but—on the other hand—I was fuming about the way I'd been taken on the stock sale. Seven months after I started, I walked into John Brown's office. "John," I said, "I've got some good news for you. I quit! And something else, John! I'm not going to let this stock thing drop, either. You're a lawyer and I trusted that you were giving me sound advice, but now I wonder and I intend to check it out."

And check it out I did. Local lawyers all thought my case against KFC was clear. But I wanted the best counsel I could get, so I hired F. Lee Bailey—one of the finest attorneys in America. He agreed to take my case on a contingency basis. He would get 10% of my stock, which would give him a market value of $200,000. I had confidence in Bailey. Shortly after Bailey filed the lawsuit against KFC, I received a phone call from John Brown. I thought Brown wasn't supposed to call me directly. I thought our lawyers should work this out. With Bailey's help, I got my stock back one month later.

My experience with John Brown and the National Diversified stock made me a little less trusting of people, especially the real smooth types. When big bucks are involved, be careful, no matter who you think you're dealing with.

Let me put it this way. You have to keep four things in mind when you're dealing in the Major Leagues.

Dave's Tips on Bumping Bellies With the Big Guys

1. *Check it out.* If someone has something big to gain on a piece of advice they give you, check it out first. Even more, don't make any big money decision based on what just one person recommends, no matter how much you might trust him.

2. *Figure out what people want you for.* After a while, it seemed to me that KFC had "parked" me in my job. I don't think John Y. Brown really cared what I was doing. What I believed he wanted was for me to turn over my National Diversified stock and not cause any trouble.

3. *Cut through the compliments.* If people compliment you and there's no reason for it, they may be after something else. Don't let glad-handing, back-slapping praise blind you to what is really going on.

4. *If you go to court, go in style.* There are plenty of lawyers who don't earn their fees or who milk a case for plenty more than they deserve. If you have to take legal action, choose a lawyer with a solid reputation and a great track record.

PART II

Part 2

6

The Business Behind the Hamburger

Well, like my adoptive dad predicted, I was out of work, and I was only thirty-seven. The only difference was that I had several million in the bank and a gold mine of an idea in my head. Quitting KFC was the first time in my adult life that I wasn't getting a paycheck. When money was needed, I just sold some of my stock so my family and I wouldn't have to forgo anything. But not getting regular wages made me nervous. When you've been poor you always have that fear that you might be poor again, and you lie awake worrying at night. I was scared.

When National Diversified called and asked me to take over operations at its Arthur Treacher's Fish and Chips restaurant chain, I felt obligated to respond. The company was now called National Fast Foods, and I was the second largest stockholder. My salary was about $20,000 a year.

The fish business never really turned me on, but it was something to do. The dream of a hamburger place was still in my head. Hamburgers were always my favorite food, and I just felt that I understood them better than anybody. Back at the Hobby Ranch House, Dick Clauss—Phil's son—and I looked at a lot of hamburger places. We'd see a store or stand or a restaurant that was a little different, and we would go in and take a look at it. We'd have a hamburger and ask a lot of questions. Phil personally knew a man in Lima, Ohio, Stubby Wilson, who had a great hamburger operation. It was called the Kewpee Hamburger Stand, and I learned a lot from it. They made hamburgers fresh off the grill and sold them as fast as they could get them out. Stubby bought beef rounds and ground his own hamburger. He was a great believer in fresh merchandise and fresh products. Stubby's ideas on hamburgers stuck in the back of my mind.

One friend of mine in particular, Len Immke, patiently listened to my hamburger dreams for hours on end. Len had an automobile dealership in town and I had bought a new Buick from him when I was with KFC. He hadn't put a lot of pressure on me, and that impressed me. He was straightforward, honest, and he knew plenty about business, especially his own. We were built kind of the same and were always fighting a weight problem, so we'd go to the Columbus Athletic Club to work out together. Each week, while we sat in the steam room, I would map out my restaurant ideas to him in detail.

"Len," I would say, "it's not how much meat you have on the bun, it's the proportion of meat to the bun. You know what I mean? A lot of people will give you a real thick hamburger, but to me, that's not really the *best* hamburger. It is a hamburger steak and a piece of bread." Len would smile and say, "You're absolutely right, Dave."

"And I would patty my fresh beef, you know, press it out in a mold because then it's more evenly cooked. It's not raw in one spot and well done in the other. That's why you cook it slowly on a grill, too. Does that make sense to you?" Len thought about it and said that sounded right, too. We'd talk and talk and get hotter just sitting there, so we'd have someone send up a pitcher of beer. So, we'd talk about hamburger restaurants and life in general, sweating in the steam room but drinking beer at the same time. Sounds kind of dumb, doesn't it?

Len's views were like Kenny King's. We both agreed that our families were the most important things we had, and that family, religion, and vocation went together. You have to have a job to support your family and you have to have religion to keep your family, job, and philosophy together. And then you have an obligation to help people who need help.

After one session, Len suggested we go to the Club dining room for a hamburger, but it was closed. Len jumped on that right away. "See, Dave, it's what I've been telling you. It's tough to get a meal downtown at the noon hour. We really ought to have a hamburger operation down here. You're always talking to me about timing. Well, if you want my opinion, the time is right, right now." By then, my job at Arthur Treacher's was getting boring, and I figured that I could get my kids educated and keep food on the table with just one successful hamburger restaurant. Believe me, the idea of a chain of restaurants was not on my mind yet.

"And I've got just the right location for you," Len said, beaming. The former New York Yankee star Tommy Hendricks had a steak house over on the corner of Broad Street. The business hadn't worked out. Len had bought the building and was using part of it for prepping new Buicks for his showroom down the street. The lounge and bar area were sitting empty. I could use that space, he said. His mechanics couldn't find a place to eat lunch. The only thing downtown was hotels, and they didn't feel welcome there in their greasy uniforms. Besides, it was too expensive. Len offered the space to me for $250 a month rent, and we shook hands. I remember him sighing and saying, "It'll be worth it if I can finally get some peace and quiet in the steam room. Do you think we can get something to eat now?" he asked.

"O.K.," I said, "but let's drive around a little bit so I can get a real feel for the area." After about an hour, when we were about a mile from downtown, Len told me to stop the car. "Pull in to that Dairy Queen over there," he said. "Len," I said, "you can't make any money with those things. I'm not stopping." "Dave," he said, "I don't want to buy the store. We still haven't had anything to eat and I just want an ice-cream cone!"

After that talk with Len, all of my thinking gelled very quickly. While traveling or just driving in my car, I'd try to think of a name for a hamburger place. My children's names came first because I wanted it to be a family business, something for them to fall back on: PAM'S, KENNY'S, MOLLY'S, MELINDA'S, LORI'S . . . but none of them seemed to be right.

To me, nothing would be a more appealing advertisement than showing a little girl, smiling and rosy-cheeked, enjoying one of my fresh, made-to-order hamburgers, but none of my daughters' names fit. Then it came to me.

When my daughter, Melinda Lou, was born, neither her brother nor her two sisters could pronounce her name. They started calling her Wenda, which then turned into Wendy. Her cleanly scrubbed, freckled face was it. I knew that was the name and the image for the business: "Wendy's." And I knew "Old Fashioned Hamburgers" had to be part of the image because that's the type of hamburger we'd serve. With the name WENDY'S and the logo of a smiling, wholesome little girl, my restaurant would be the place where you went for a hamburger the way you used to get them, with fresh, pure American beef. My experience with the Colonel taught me the importance of image and of having a personal identity tied to the restaurant.

Wendy's was born at a time when nostalgia was sweeping the country. I wanted to offer a warm but simple family atmosphere, with upscale overtones, so the interior of my store featured carpeting, Tiffany lamps, hanging beads, old-fashioned advertising on the tabletops, and bentwood chairs. The crew was dressed in traditional "whites," which gave the feel of cleanliness and tradition. The women wore white dresses and scarves, and the men wore white pants, white shirt, a black bow tie, and chef's hat. Everyone wore white aprons.

The menu for Wendy's would be limited and simple. A single hamburger would go for 55 cents, a double for 95 cents, and a triple, with ¾ pound of meat, for $1.35. Thick and meaty chili cost 55 cents, a creamy, smooth Frosty, 35 cents, french fries, 30 cents, and assorted beverages ranged from 15 cents to 25 cents. My angle was that at Wendy's you could get hamburgers served the way you liked them because of the many ways you could mix the condiments. The customer could come up with hundreds of combinations, but the menu itself was super narrow. The only item on the original menu that we got rid of was sugar cream pie at 40 cents a slice. Why? Because I kept on eating it all, and we'd forever be running out for the customer.

Wendy's stuck with my original menu for ten years, but it was a fight to keep it that way because there was always pressure to add more items. I'd come up with ideas. Everyone else would, too; but we hung tough. To this day, I believe that most entrepreneurs—especially in the restaurant business—get into trouble by making their menus too broad and offering too many products.

Before we opened, my biggest worry was the view held by serious business people that the fast-food industry was saturated, and the last thing that America needed was another hamburger restaurant. Every day, there'd be articles in *The*

Wall Street Journal or some other business publication about new fast-food places. To me, hamburgers made to order and made from fresh meat made all the difference. My friends Len Immke, Ron Musick, Kenny King, and Bob Barney—who hooked up with me at KFC—supported me 100%. Wendy's would work, I knew, if the product was made fast enough and costs were controlled.

I always preach about having a plan, but, ironically, I really didn't have a plan for Wendy's when I started out. What I had was a concept and plenty of operating experience, but there was no five-year plan with a restaurant-opening schedule or a financing program. There was nothing like that at all. For the sake of drama, I wish I could tell you that it was more complicated than that, but it wasn't.

On November 15, 1969, I did a lot of praying. That was the day we opened the first Wendy's. We had three full-time employees. Gloria Ward Soffe, who still works for me today, was bookkeeper, chili maker, and register operator.

A crowd of Columbus dignitaries—including the mayor—and a number of suppliers came to the opening party. The hit of the evening was little eight-year-old Wendy. Lorraine made her a long blue-and-white striped dress, and styled her hair, sprayed it, and put pipe cleaners into her pigtails to make them stick out. On the end of each pigtail, Lorraine tied two blue bows. About midway through the party, I felt a tug on my jacket. Wendy looked at me, pigtails drooping and said, "Daddy, I've been smiling so much, like you told me to, that my mouth hurts now."

From that first day forward, Wendy has been a great spokesperson for the company. When she was sixteen she gave a speech to fifteen hundred people at our annual convention. She's lost some of her privacy because she's been tied so closely to the company. While in school at the University of

Florida, she got plenty of letters from guys who had hopes, she says, "of marrying her dad's wallet." (Relax, guys. Wendy and Paul are happily married, have a youngster, Amanda, and now have a Wendy's franchise.) Because some people still take her for the official company spokesperson, sometimes she hedges speaking her mind. I don't blame her.

The first day we opened our doors for business, customers were lined up down the street, and the business caught on right from the start. Like Len Immke said, the time was right. But why? Because the market was ripe for the business. The opening of Wendy's wasn't backed up with fancy market research, but I had a nose for trends in the restaurant business. (Research isn't everything. Not long after we started, Burger King paid a lot of money for a research study that explained why Wendy's wouldn't work.) Now, I can look back and tell you what those trends were. Back in 1969, these were feelings in my gut. They would have been tough to put into words then, but let me try now.

The Secrets of Sniffing Around

1. *People wanted choices.* This was the time of Vietnam. People were rebelling against everything. Some big segments of the population were tiring of a prepackaged world, including the stuff they were getting at McDonald's. They wanted some influence over what they were buying. Also, people were doing a lot of experimenting. They wanted something new.

2. *People were fed up with poor quality.* There was a big drive for things natural and wholesome, the way people remembered them being before World War II. Today's baby boomers were then just becoming young adults and discovering their taste buds. They wanted better alternatives.

3. *People were adjusting to a new, more complicated way of life.* So many changes were going on—the Vietnam war, computers, the stress of modern-day life. The young adults were after something that was "totally radical," while their parents just wanted the kids to turn down their stereos and stay in school. The parents wanted a simpler time and traditional values. In a funny way, the old-fashioned decor and the Tiffany lamps provided a novelty for the young adults and nostalgia for the older generation at the same time.

4. *People were on the move.* That's why the Pick-Up window was so important. Drive-ins had lost popularity, and nobody had figured out how to deliver a custom sandwich through a pick-up window. It's interesting that this is one part of the business that we didn't perfect right away. At first, Wendy's succeeded as a restaurant, not a carryout spot. However, when we got the pickup right, it was such a powerful advantage that it allowed us to franchise the business fast.

5. *People were ready for an upscale hamburger place.* Plenty of people were like me. They grew up loving hamburgers, but they didn't like what they got at most fast-food places, where the food was designed for kids and teenagers who really didn't care what they were eating.

Knowing these five trends allowed Wendy's to focus on the right market. My bet is that if you looked at any successful business, you would find factors very much like these behind that business's success. If you're going to bet your bankroll on a business concept, you had better be able to understand those forces. If you can't describe them, you have to feel them so clearly in your gut that you *know* you're right.

We began our operations on a small scale to test how the idea would work. I knew we had to crawl before we tried to walk. Wendy's started making money after six weeks in business. Before then, our whole focus was just on what we needed to break even. Then it became clear that the idea had definite potential. In November 1970 I opened the second Wendy's restaurant in the suburbs. It was important to see if the ideas would work in a second location and if it could work in the suburbs. You had to know if the first success was just a fluke. I was still working at Arthur Treacher's at the time and bought some land on Henderson Road. It was the first Wendy's with a Pick-Up window, but it took a while to perfect that. It was then that Ron Musick and Bob Barney joined me from Arthur Treacher's. I told them that I didn't have enough business to justify adding them to the payroll, so we would have to open more stores. And, I warned them they might end up working the grill or running the register during the lunch rush. That was no joke. Road construction in front of the second restaurant had taken such a bite out of sales, I was funding some of the payroll out of my savings account.

Bob and Ron became shareholders in the second store. Many company founders go down the drain being greedy. If you want to build your company, you have to deal your key people in. If you take care of everyone who is working hard to help you, you take care of yourself. An organization is able to grow and profit when the key people share in the future, when you tell your people that this is their company, too.

Right off the bat, I offered Bob Barney ten shares of stock and Ron Musick five shares at $100 a share. It was like the deal that Phil Clauss had cut with me earlier. All Ron had was $250, so he asked me to give him a year to pay off the remaining $250 at 6% interest. When Ron had the money to pay for his stock, he was one of the happiest people I had ever seen. And today, those five shares have brought him and his family considerable pride and comfort. At the beginning, though, it meant sharing in the risk.

We merged the first and second Wendy's together into one

company. When we went down to Bank One to borrow money for new equipment packages, eight of us—four co-owners and our wives—had to sign the notes individually. Ron was living in an apartment in Worthington and would bring home these $150,000 notes to sign. His wife would ask: "What would happen if this thing doesn't work?" Ron would say, "All we have is a car and a 'partment. If they want those, then we lose 'em. And that's all they get, 'cause they won't take bodies."

In 1971 we decided to go for two more stores in lower- to middle-income neighborhoods where Wendy's hamburgers were clearly higher priced than the competition. This was a tough test, but both stores opened to company records of around $10,000 a week. We knew then that we really had something. It was no longer a matter of *if* we were going to make it, but *how big* it was going to be.

In June of 1972, we opened our first Wendy's outside of Ohio (in Indianapolis). We did it to establish ourselves in interstate trade and commerce. That let us protect our trademarks and copyrights. And it was then that I left my job at Arthur Treacher's and turned all of my energies toward Wendy's. By this time, the company had more than doubled in size. Wendy's was on its way.

Go Open One Up— Dave's Checklist for Getting Into Business

When people ask me how to start a small business, I say: "Go open one up." Then grind it out. Make a profit. No one wants to hear that, but it's true. Nobody's going to tell you anything worth hearing until the customer tells you at the cash register.

Pete Boinis, a good friend of mine and a true innovator in the restaurant industry, has a very sound philosophy about starting a business. He says innovation comes first, but after innovation, two other factors are just as important: motivation and realism. If you don't know how to attract and motivate the best people, it's not likely the business will get off the ground. If the business can only succeed if everything goes 100% as planned, forget it; it won't go anywhere either. You have to have all three ingredients.

Lots of people come to me with ideas for business deals. They want my advice, but most of the time, they want my money, too. The first question I always ask is, "What's your plan?" Remember, I didn't have a formal plan. I also wasn't asking anyone to invest in me, either. That's a big difference. If you want investors, you better have a plan you can spell out and it better be convincing. The plan can be exciting and original, but it's even more important that the person behind it be totally committed.

1. *Are you willing to go open one up?* A guy who worked for me opened up a sandwich-and-ice-cream place. He had a possibility. I told him to work at it and make a profit. But, he had a fantasy: He wanted to be big right away. His costs were too high, and he didn't make any money. Like so many start-ups, he wanted to be a chain overnight. Wendy's made a profit by the sixth week it was in business, but it wasn't a lot of money. Use the first place you open to learn everything you can about how the business works. Most important, will people actually pay money for your product or service?

2. *Do you know how your personal plan meshes with your business?* What's your goal? Are you really challenged by this idea, or is it just something to do? What do you want to achieve? How do you feel about working long hours? How much knowledge and experience do you have in the business you are planning to start? How much of your own money do you have on the line?

Are you really ready to do what you want to do? It's all in the timing. Timing includes having all the education, all the on-the-job training, and all the knowledge about that business that you'll need to succeed. And then there is a certain feeling inside that tells you when you are ready. You just know it.

Now, it's O.K. to change your mind. You don't have to have the same plan your whole life, but you have to have a plan. And, at any point in time, you have to be truly serious about that plan.

3. *How much will you sacrifice?* A lot of people think they're ready, but they get trapped. They work for a company and can't afford to make changes because their standard of living is too high and they won't give anything up. Sometimes they pay for a big promotion for the rest of their life because they lose control. They have to join country clubs, buy a bigger car and a bigger house. Each thing takes more money. It's not the original cost; it's the upkeep of maintaining the life-style! When a person is ready for a change he has to pick a point and stop. He has to be honest with himself and ask, What do I really want to do and can I do it? Am I willing to put everything I have at risk? How much would I and maybe my family have to give up to make a new start? Does my family understand the risks as well as I do? How will it feel to live in a world without pensions and profit sharing? A world with limited expense accounts and no bonuses? A world without company cars or the status of being with an established company?

The most important thing you'll have to sacrifice is time. You can't start a new business sitting in an armchair. Your tennis game will probably go to hell. You can forget about a vacation, or if you get one, it'll probably last no more than a couple of days. And your family life may well suffer . . . but that can be worked out if they support you and you are committed to supporting them.

4. *Do you have enough confidence to succeed?* Sometimes, people are ready and qualified but they haven't got the confidence. Mainly, you look at the experience you have and how successfully you have performed. But you better know what is driving you, too. Give yourself good reasons why you really want to do something and tell yourself that you CAN make it happen.

5. *Are you willing to stay small until you really have it right?* If a small business person was just starting out in a new concept strategy, the thing that any smart investor or bank will want to know is if you are going to stay small until you get your organization together. It's the "I'm going to operate this out of my house" attitude, and "I'm not going to have any overhead." Don't hire people until you can afford them. Once you hire them, you may end up paying them out of your own pocket if the business falters. Or you could lose them as friends or business partners forever.

6. *Are you focused on the right things?* I remember watching the TV show "Moonlighting" with Cybill Shepherd. In it she plays a model—Maddie Hayes—who takes over a detective agency and has gorgeous offices overnight. That's not the way it works when you open a business. The biggest mistake small businesses can make is to build fancy offices. Offices are one of the worst things in the world. But I shouldn't talk. Today we have beautiful offices. Mine overlooks a miniature garden and it has fancy paneling. There are also two handsome chairs by the desk, which Duke University and Ohio State presented to me . . . in honor of the fact, they said, that they could never find a seat in our restaurants. Wiseguys.

• • •

As attractive and as well designed as our Wendy's head-quarters offices are, sometimes I wonder if they are justified even today. If I were a bank, I would never lend money to a little company with fancy offices, really and truly.

We had the most fun—let me tell you—at our office over on Henderson Road. It was packed. The glass company, Anchor Hocking, was there, as were a couple of doctors, Coca-Cola, and Wendy's. Some of us sat out in the hall. We also took care of the whole building's janitorial services. Sometimes, a painter would come in and do a sloppy job for one of the tenants. They'd get upset and leave . . . and I didn't try to stop them. After all, we needed the space. On some days, one of us would come back to the office with $200,000–300,000 in franchise fees, which we would drop off in the hallway until we could deposit it in the bank. We had a picnic trying to run things in that maze, but it worked.

Focus is so important, and YOU HAVE TO HAVE FOCUS IN EVERY PART OF YOUR BUSINESS.

- Do you have a clear focus on who your customer is?
- Do you have a sharp focus on your product and where it fits among all the other competing products out there in the marketplace?
- Do you have a focus on how you will operate your business, and do you know it so well and so clearly that you can explain it to others and motivate those people to do their jobs?

Here's another example of focus: I was a partner in buying a manufacturing company with about one hundred customers that did about $3 million in sales annually. It was losing money. We cut the customers down to ten and the volume down to $1 million. Today we turn a nice profit on $25 million in sales. It's a trim shop. We do a lot of sewing and leather work for companies like Honda. But we would be out of business today if we didn't actually limit the number of customers we worked for. There is no way that we could have the capacity to serve everybody.

7. *Do you have a good handle on the key expenses?* A first-time operator just launching a business has to be real careful about the amount of money that he sinks into real estate. You can't lock it all up in the location and then have no money to operate with. You need to know all your key costs down to the penny.

8. *Do you know about local or national issues that could help or hurt your business?* This is a bigger and bigger concern today, but it was big even when we first opened Wendy's. For example, zoning really limited where we could go, and that's what caused all the quick-service restaurants to be clustered in little pockets. Today, you have to figure out what your business does to the environment, or if you'll be able to get qualified workers. There are plenty of traps to steer clear of. A mail-order business better know what will happen to postage rates for the next five years. You have to watch out for issues that don't seem like they are part of your business operations right now because they can have a real impact later on.

9. *Do you have your suppliers lined up?* You better have great relationships with your suppliers. Ed Ourant, who is now an executive vice president and one of our top operations people, was a franchisee for several other chains at the time I started Wendy's. He really had connections and helped our people get the right suppliers, and that can be worth gold. You may want to go with cheaper suppliers, but you can pay a big price for that. At first, we had the wrong cups. (We

called them "leakers.") We also had some problems in distribution. Ed straightened us out.

10. *Are all the legal bases covered?* When a little company starts up, there are always lots of handshake deals everywhere. They say entrepreneurs hate lawyers and I'm an entrepreneur, but if I had one thing to do differently when I opened up Wendy's, it would be to involve lawyers more often. You better get the best legal advice because we live in a legal world, and you need to have the best legal advice you can possibly buy.

John Casey, our vice chairman and chief financial officer, is a rare blend of wisdom, common sense, and negotiating skill. John is a lawyer who can put a conflict to bed faster than any manager I know. It was John who taught me that you had to involve lawyers in certain things. You have to protect yourself if people or circumstances don't turn out as you expect. A lawyer can also protect you from your own mistakes. No matter what happens, my advice is simple: Don't get greedy! But don't give your rights away either, and find a lawyer (if you can) who believes both ideas because they are your negotiators if things don't work out. You have to trust them to clean up conflict . . . but be sure they have common sense, not just a lot of two-dollar words.

11. *Are you ready to deal with the banks?* I sure wasn't when I took over the KFC restaurants in Columbus. One of the first things I wanted to do was to install air-conditioning systems in the four restaurants because I know how air conditioning could build traffic. But, instead of going downtown to the commercial loan department and talking with somebody who knew something about business, I went to the local branch that did our banking. The loan office there knew about loans for cars and refrigerators but couldn't understand air conditioning as a business principle. Instead of a loan, what I got

was a big lecture on how late these restaurants were in paying their bills and what a lousy risk I was.

My early experiences left me pretty sour on banks and the judgment of bankers. With the savings-and-loan scandal, the junk-bond fiasco, and more banks teetering near the brink of bankruptcy, it's difficult for the businessman to maintain confidence in his bank. That hurts the spirit of entrepreneurship and America's system of free enterprise.

There are many fine people in the banking industry, but some of the bad apples in banking have done plenty of harm. To me, it's a big sin when a bank lends money to people who are poor risks and who aren't likely to pay it back. Every bank should—and the best banks DO—ask the question: "How will you make your payments if things go sour?"

A small businessperson needs a good banker to survive and to expand the company. When you pick a banker, don't go after the one with the fanciest computer system or the slickest brochure. Pick a bank with experience in dealing with small businesses and a banker with a good sense of business judgment.

As for me, I've always tried to do business banking in a very simple way:

- Pay the bills on time.
- Put more weight on the cash balance rather than on "cash flow" and other fancy bookkeeping.
- Learn which banking people you should call on.
- Always take a clear, sensible business plan with you whenever you ask a bank for money.
- Pick a bank with a reputation for standing by its customers. (One who won't forget you.)

Does this checklist scare you? It should, and it only lists some of the most important things you have to worry about when you go into business for yourself. I'm the last person to DIS-COURAGE anyone from going into business for themselves, but I'm also the FIRST person to encourage people to go into business the right way.

If all this sounds like too much risk and a little beyond what you can do right now, *and* you still want to be your own boss to some extent, maybe you want to consider being a franchisee. Franchising is a middle ground between working for someone else and starting your own business from scratch. A franchisor gives you the right to market goods or services under a trade name like Wendy's. In exchange for this, the franchisor (let's say it's Wendy's) gets an initial payment for the franchise, a certain percentage of the sales (called royalties), and some fees as well. It also gets to inspect and control the quality of the operations so that it can protect the quality and reputation that goes behind the franchise brand. That's very important for this reason: If you're a Wendy's customer, you want to know that you can get the same great Wendy's quality at whatever Wendy's you visit. That's what being a well-managed chain is all about. In addition to the right to sell under our name, franchisees also get company systems, training programs, buying discounts through mass purchasing, and advice on managing their business.

Franchising is a low-cost way to become your own boss. Although about 75% of independent businesses fail within the first two years, the failure rate for franchises is less than 10%. Franchising is what Wendy's is all about. Of the 4,000 Wendy's restaurants, about 1,150 are owned directly by Wendy's, and the rest are franchises. We have three hundred international franchises in places as far off as Turkey, Japan, and Guatemala. Our franchisees are our biggest customers, and what they buy from us is the Wendy's concept . . . defined down to the smallest detail.

Anybody considering the franchise route should check the franchise out very carefully. If I were looking to buy a franchise today, this is what I would do and the kind of questions I would ask. I want you to know that this checklist mentions Wendy's a lot. We aren't always the best at everything we do, but we're good, and the Wendy's system is the one I know best. There are plenty of fine franchises out there . . . in restaurants and in other businesses, too.

How to Check a Franchise Out

1. *Read everything you can about the franchisor.* Go to the library and read through the trade and business magazines. If you have a stockbroker, call him or her up and see if they have any investment research on the company. Ask for the annual report from the company.

2. *See the business work.* Visit franchise operations in action. Always look at several different units and see how well the standards hold up from one place to the next. Is one place sloppy and slow, while the other is sharp and fast? If you find big differences, the system could be weak, and that could be a problem.

3. *Talk with other franchisees.* What do they like about the franchise? What don't they like? Does the franchisor make good on its commitments? Is the franchisor a tough inspector of its operations? (Believe me, you want them to be because that keeps the value of the franchise up.) Do the franchisees get straight talk from headquarters? Does headquarters give the franchisees strong programs to help motivate employees? Is there much difference between franchised and company-owned units? In the best franchise companies, you will sense

very little or no difference between a company-owned unit and a franchisee.

4. *Learn about the backgrounds of other franchisees.* I definitely think it's better to be tied up with a franchisor where the franchisees actually operate the business rather than where they are just investors. When a franchisee applies to do business, we look at their financial qualifications, but mainly we look at who's going to operate the business.

Back at the beginning of Wendy's, franchisees had all kinds of backgrounds. Doctors, lawyers, accountants, oil people, you name it. We just had them flocking in here. But, they really didn't have operating experience. As the industry got more competitive, it got crystal clear that only experienced operators could survive. A franchisee couldn't say, "I'm just putting up the money to run this thing and open the doors." You can't hire out everything that needs to be done. We call that an absentee-run show. And it's a zero.

We have told some franchisees, some excellent people, to please leave the business. A franchise isn't just an investment, it's a way of life. You can't play this game from the sidelines. You have to be there to tell your managers every day, "You're really doing a good job." That lifts a person so high, and it's how you get superior performance. If you can't tell them that, something's wrong.

Today, although Wendy's is still by far the biggest thing in my business life, I'm not involved in the day-to-day operations. I have other investments. But when I was turning around those KFC stores in Columbus, it was all Kentucky Fried Chicken. When Wendy's was ready to expand, I was 100% Wendy's. Again, it comes back to focus.

The operators of the franchises come in all sizes, by the way. An operator can have one unit or a hundred. If you can, you should find out if the franchisor handles the big and small operators differently and in what ways. If you're a single-unit franchisee, will you be taken seriously, or are you just a fly speck?

5. *Find out what the franchisor does to help communications.* Go for a franchisor that throws good regional meetings or conventions. Not so you can wear funny hats or sit on whoopee cushions, but so there is a chance to get together and share information. When I say GOOD CONVENTION, I mean one where there is good dialogue and where the communication flows more than the booze. Franchisees get more out of talking with each other than you can imagine. In Wendy's case, they talk about how they handle labor and food costs, recruiting, and retention, and how new menu items are doing. A franchisee should leave a convention with a mental checklist of how to inventory his operations, not with a hangover.

When you buy into a franchise, one of the most important things you're buying is the network to the other franchisees and to headquarters. They should have an open line and an open door back at headquarters so you can lick problems fast. Be wary of a franchise organization whose channels of communications are so complicated that no one can ever get through to the top people.

6. *Study the company's stand on pricing its franchises.* The average investment for land, building, and equipment for a Wendy's started out at about $200,000. The average number of units per franchise was between ten and twenty because we franchised entire territories rather than individual units. In 1985, the investment rose to between $600,000 and $1 million. Today, a Wendy's restaurant costs between $800,000 and $1.2 million.

It's real important to keep the cost of a new franchise moderately priced. We want to get in as cheap as possible, because it goes in on the overhead and you want to keep overhead down so you can make a profit. The franchise has to be within the reach of the operators, not the investors. The bigger franchise operations also have programs to help minorities and women get into franchises on favorable terms. We do at Wendy's.

I'd be super cautious about buying a franchise in a real small chain. Just to be a franchise with two or three stores is dumb. There ought to be a law against that, because you've got to give your franchisees something for their money and with two or three units you just can't afford to. If the chain has just a couple of units, then it should at least have a plan for rapid expansion.

Although I didn't have an expansion plan when I built the first Wendy's, we had very clear plans once we began franchising the business. I knew I had to move fast because I wanted to build a national business. That meant national TV advertising if we were to compete with Burger King or McDonald's. The only way I could get the money was by building more restaurants. To do that fast we had to offer franchises. Our first franchise restaurant opened in March of 1972, in Marion, Ohio—about three-and-a-half years after we had opened the first Wendy's and only after the concept was completely tested out. Sometimes I signed up as many as four or five franchisees in a single day. In 1974, on any given day, you could walk into our offices and see twenty to thirty men with briefcases waiting to see us.

Franchise relationships is another area where Bob Barney helped me through his follow-up. He worked at building the system and keeping the standards that came from rapid expansion. We were moving like a jet plane down the runway—a thousand restaurants in one hundred months and the first hamburger chain to achieve $1 billion in sales in its first ten years.

7. *Find out what the franchisor has done when a franchisee gets into trouble.* The most important thing here is communication. Usually, when a franchisee gets into trouble, it happens slowly. Sales taper off gradually. The building gets run down bit by bit. About a year ago, this happened to one of our franchisees in Ohio. He didn't even want to meet with us when we came through his town on a visit. Maybe he was embarrassed. Maybe he was mad. When we put our heads together, we were able to convince him to invest $10,000 in renovations. As a result, he doubled his business in a year. The key is the communications, so you can find out about the problem before it goes too far.

8. *Learn if there are any additional "hidden" charges you'll be obliged to pay.* We do not sell our franchise owners anything except the rights to our name and trademarks and our proven concept. We do have a bakery operation, but franchisees don't have to buy from us. They DO have to buy under our specifications.

We had learned some important lessons from running franchises because of the experiences we had at Kentucky Fried Chicken and Arthur Treacher's. We wanted our agreements to be fair. To us, that also meant steering clear of:

- selling equipment
- selling food products
- owning commissaries
- distributing products

The proof that our way was right, I think, was the number of owners who signed up with us who had already been franchisees with other restaurant businesses.

Plenty of franchise operators have gotten into trouble because they force their franchisees to buy supplies or equipment from them. The franchisees end up owing a lot of money to the franchisor. The resentment starts when the franchisor spends lots of money on new products and equipment, and the little franchisee is sitting there trying to make the payments on everything.

Franchisees should pay a franchisor to have their problems solved, not to be sold a bunch of merchandise. The franchise support services we offer at Wendy's include operations (training, quality control, business consulting); marketing; site selection; engineering; purchasing; and finance consultation.

9. *Consider working for the company before you buy one of their franchises.* More and more people come to work at Wendy's hoping to buy a franchise one day. That's really the best thing for the company, too, because the franchisee gets to learn the system from the inside. At Wendy's, many people who have been here over ten years have an opportunity to get a franchise.

Working with franchisees has been a big part of my life in the last twenty years. It's been exciting and fun.

Without franchising, Wendy's could never have expanded so rapidly. From the beginning we've looked at our franchisees as our number one customers. Because the average return on investment we delivered was so high, it also encouraged the banks to lend franchisees money so they in turn could build quickly in the territories they were granted.

Being a Wendy's operator has changed many people's lives. A few weeks back, I went to a company operators' banquet in West Virginia. This particular group had been having a tough time a couple of years back because convenience food stores and plenty of other competitors were cutting into their business. But they turned it around. One woman came up to me and said she spent $385 on her dress so she could see me and come to that banquet. It was more money than she ever thought she'd spend on a dress in her life. She looked great. She was beaming and proud. And that's no bull. I was embarrassed that this woman would spend that kind of money because I'm sure not worth it. But I was proud, too, because this was her life, and she was succeeding at it. We were supposed to get back to the airport at nine, but we got so wrapped up talking to people that we didn't leave until much later.

When you become a franchisor like Wendy's, you have a tremendous responsibility. Remember, I was a stakeholder in a franchise, too, for more than a decade with Kentucky Fried Chicken. So I know what it's like from the franchisee side. Franchises are valuable, and it's right to expect franchisees to work hard for the money they make. But a franchisee is also a customer . . . and a human being. Often a franchisee has raised the money for the franchise by borrowing on his house or on the savings for the kids' education. You have to be sure that the franchisee who goes out and risks his or her money, buys a franchise, and works hard is going to be successful. It's a two-way deal, and you've got to have a two-way attitude.

7

Giving Customers Choices

A grill that's set at 2-5-0,
With meat and cheese that's ready to go . . .

From the front to the back, you got to lay it down,
Place 'em evenly, not scattered around . . .

Press top to bottom, left to right,
and you'll get a patty that's outta sight!

THE PATTY CHORUS: We start to shrink,
When we hit that grill, you know we will.
You know we will, when we hit that grill!

We don't have a company song at Wendy's. Yet. But, we do have some super training videos, like "Grill Skills." The rap-song lyrics up above come from that tape. Every trainee who wants to learn how to cook hamburgers has to see the video and get the pattern down perfect. In a business that depends on operations, every job or task has to have a rhythm and a pace to it. Ours is no exception.

A Wendy's grillperson really has to be a master of the four-corner press. A four-corner press has nothing to do with basketball or bench-pressing. It's a routine for using the grill spatula to press out the fat and seal in the flavor when cooking a Wendy's hamburger. It has to work like clockwork because the grill cooks our hamburger in about four minutes.

We take grilling very seriously. We have contests to select the best grillperson in each restaurant. Whoever wins gets the title of Top Grill, which is the Wendy's version of the Air Force's Top Gun. You see, although the hamburger takes four minutes to cook, we aim to get it to the customer within fifteen seconds after it's ordered. To do that, you have to constantly have hamburgers "staged" at various states of wellness with the right number of hamburgers to serve as customers place their orders. The grillman has to figure all this out.

A few years back, I was walking through one of our kitchens and told a kid in Cincinnati—big kid, Arnold Schwarzenegger size—"You're not four-corner pressing. The hamburgers won't look right, and they won't taste right, either. We want the last bite to be every bit as good as the first." Well, the kid just took his spatula, laid the next set of patties on the grill, and turned to me and said, "O.K., you do it, Big Shot!" So, guess what? I'm the grillman. I did it. You have to prove yourself. I showed him how to choke up on the spatula like a Louisville Slugger, and he really got the hang of it. Meanwhile, somebody came up and called me "Mr. Thomas," and the grillman figured out who I was. "Sorry about the 'Big Shot,'" he apologized. "Don't worry about it, son," I said, looking up at him. "Coming from you it was a compliment."

I didn't like being called Big Shot, but I did like getting straight talk. I'm at a disadvantage today. I'm so well known through the TV advertising that I can't go into a Wendy's unnoticed. People want to make an impression on me. They run around mopping and polishing and smiling so much, you know it can't be real, even for Wendy's. So I sometimes don't see the real world.

A restaurant is like a little factory, and a menu item is really a product for us. I don't think it lessens Wendy's or any other restaurant to compare it to a factory. Porsche sports cars and Rolex watches are made in factories, too! In a restaurant "factory," the raw materials come in the back door and the finished product is served at the front counter. That's as true for the swankiest joint in Manhattan as it is for the Wendy's in Ashtabula, Ohio. The goal is to make a product so good that people will tell others about the terrific experience they just had. We preach to our people: "You should always make the hamburger you'd be proud to serve to your best friend."

A restaurant concept—like being a seafood place or specializing in desserts—doesn't make a restaurant business. Anybody can come up with a restaurant concept. Entrepreneurs who get into the restaurant business think that it's their secret recipe for clam chowder or lemon pie that will make them rich and let them build a chain operation. It isn't a question of knowing how to make a french fry. It's a question of making four thousand units to make them the same right way day after day. The concept is important, but the management of operations is way more important.

The same goes for people already in the business. Adding a brand-new item won't save a stumbling restaurant. Too many people want to hit a home run with the latest fad menu item rather than have a sparkling, clean restroom. We are always getting ideas for new products from managers: alfalfa sprouts on hamburgers, Cajun hamburgers, ham on toasted muffins. There's no end. But, as I say again and again, "The salad bar won't wash your windows." Well-managed operations are more important than any one product you sell.

A very young Dave Thomas with Grandma Minnie Sinclair. My fondest childhood memories are of the times I spent with her.

A young boy and his dreams—I was probably thinking about hamburgers!

My Army experience taught me how to make the most out of every situation, good or bad.

I started working at the Regas Restaurant in Knoxville, Tennessee, at the age of 12. I worked all night on 12-hour shifts waiting on customers at the counter at right.

Cooking with barbeque is hard work! The hickory ember pits at the Hobby Ranch House would fill up with smoke and force you out of the kitchen. That's me on the right, filling a dinner order with coworker Omar Wuthrich.

My 1954 wedding to Lorraine Buskirk marked the beginning of a loving relationship that's still going strong after 37 years.

PHOTOS COURTESY LLOYD MARQUART

Colonel Harland Sanders taught me all about promotion. Here we are at the Ohio State Fair with the Grand Champion chickens. I used to wear the string tie until people started asking me what band I played in!

Pretty 8-year-old Melinda Lou (Wendy) Thomas embodied the image I wanted for a restaurant that offered old-fashioned hamburgers.

The original Wendy cameo was created in 1969. It hasn't changed since, although we added "Quality Is Our Recipe" arched over her head a year later.

Bumping bellies with the big boys...a hamburger cook goes "Hollywood" with Danny Thomas and Frank Sinatra during the filming of "Young and Foolish," a TV show that helped raise money for St. Jude's Children's Research Hospital.

Dr. Norman Vincent Peale, a great man of God and someone I truly admire, honored me by presenting me with the Horatio Alger Award in 1979. This award was a dream come true.

Clara Peller took America by storm when she bellowed these famous words: "Where's the beef?" The former manicurist starred in the most memorable TV commercial in history.

To R. David Thomas
With best wishes, Guy Bush

I really admire President Bush for standing up for his convictions. He honored me by asking my help in raising awareness for adoption, through a campaign called "Adoption Works...For Everyone."

Adoption *does* work...just ask Barbara Gellerstein, who starred with me in a public service announcement for adoption.

The Thomas family: That's Lorraine, center, and then, clockwise from left, Wendy, Lori, Kenny, Molly, and Pam. They've given me a lifetime of love that keeps on growing—nine grandchildren and counting!

Most customers are curious about a new menu item and are usually willing to give it a try. But a good restaurant operator is very cautious about adding a new item unless it's been carefully tested. You really have to persuade the best operators that a new item is right, because a smart operator is always asking: "How is it going to work? How are my people in ten or maybe a hundred different locations going to create this product the same way day after day?"

For example, some of our operators were hesitant when we introduced our grilled chicken sandwich. They didn't think there would be enough room on the grill for both the chicken and the ground beef. They didn't want to risk mixing the flavors. We worked around it by putting a strip down the center of the grill, which actually creates two grills. I prefer operators who balk at changes and adding new products that aren't thoroughly tested.

Remember that a new product doesn't fall out of a package. It means training. For us, it also has to work all over the U.S. We do allow some regional differences to match local market tastes. We offer coleslaw in some of our Super Bars, but not in others. The sauce for our barbecue sandwiches is milder in New York than it is in Texas. But we don't overdo this.

The History Lesson in Wendy's Menu

Not too long ago, I took all the Wendy's menus from day one and laid them side by side. By doing that, you come up with an interesting history lesson about how far Wendy's and the quick-service food industry have come. You also see how the Wendy's menu—which has always had strong appeal with adults—has grown up as people's tastes have gotten more sophisticated.

You really have to start back with the McDonald brothers. I owe a big debt to McDonald's. They set me up. By that I mean they gave me something to look good against.

It all started back in the early fifties when the McDonald brothers were having labor problems in their restaurants. They thought, "Why not make this self-service?" They put some windows in and got rid of the plates and the silverware. Many restaurant operators just got tired of the personnel problems, and constantly hiring chefs and service people. What made the change possible was breakthroughs in equipment. The Colonel's Merrimac cookers let you do chicken in thirty minutes versus the then normal time of four hours. In the fifties, Ray Kroc, who bought the business and really made McDonald's, sold the brothers milkshake machines, which let you make several shakes at once. McDonald's developed a scoop that gave you the same uniform serving size of french fries no matter who handled it. With each improvement, the skill level you needed in the operation went down.

McDonald's did a tremendous job with marketing, and that's what built their business. Back in the late fifties, I saw my first McDonald's in Fort Wayne. The tiny hamburger didn't impress me. It takes a certain percentage of meat to make a good sandwich. Instead, McDonald's impressed me with two things: their real estate and their potatoes. They had great locations, and when they first began, they did their french fries with fresh potatoes, and were they good.

Some people have convictions about the making of fine silver. Others have convictions about how to run universities. I had convictions about hamburgers that came from my experiences as a kid. It's simple: A prewrapped, production sandwich is always a mistake. It's the wrong thing to do. If it sits there sweating under a heat lamp with the ketchup and mustard already spread on, it will never be as good as one that's freshly made. The whole premise of McDonald's was price—

to offer a 15-cent hamburger when hamburgers were selling for 35 and 40 cents. Of course, you could hardly find the hamburger for the pickle. It was a pocketbook issue and had nothing to do with quality or real value. I was never sold on McDonald's, Burger Chef, Burger King, or Hardee's. Even Burger King wasn't cooking to order. It was premaking and then heating sandwiches up. Since I was against premade sandwiches, I never wanted to be a franchisee with any of these companies.

So, the first three things that bothered me were: the size of their sandwich, the fact that it was prepackaged, and that it was not customized. The fourth thing I thought was wrong was the impression these fast-food stores made. Most of these places were takeout stands, not restaurants. The message they were sending to the customer was: "Here are your choices, hurry up and pay us, and get out of here because we don't have a dining room."

So, the Wendy's hamburger, the cornerstone of our menu, needed four special qualities to compete against the other chains:

1. *It had to be a real hamburger.* It doesn't cost any more in labor to make a cheap hamburger than a quality one, so labor isn't an issue. We use only fresh, 100% pure beef and we cook it at a low temperature. When it's cooking, we press in the flavor and we press out the fat.

Each patty weighs a quarter pound and is properly proportioned to the bun. In fact, we designed the patty so that the edges would stick out over the sides of the bun. That sent a message to people about how big it was—what Grandma Minnie said about not cutting corners. We also made it square because I wanted to patty our meat. Pattying keeps the looseness in the meat. Also, when you load up the grill, you can get more square patties on it. (Later, we added the two-ounce hamburger to the menu, to offer a size parents wanted, chiefly for their kids.)

We put the triple (three patties in one sandwich) on the menu, even though it wasn't ordered much, to let people know we were a place that could take care of a really big appetite. (I have a confession to make: I've never eaten a triple. The triple really helped build demand for the double. It was outrageous; the double—a reasonable compromise.)

2. *It had to be made fresh.* The basic requirements for a Wendy's hamburger are: (1) the meat must be fresh and hot; (2) the condiments must be kept cold, and (3) the meat must not touch the bun until the hamburger is sold.

I didn't think that Wendy's could succeed unless we offered only fresh meat and fresh toppings. I didn't want to get into lettuce and tomato, afraid that those choices might slow up the sandwich maker. Shredded lettuce was definitely out. It doesn't have a quality appearance . . . or flavor. It was going to be whole leaves or nothing. When you use a whole leaf it better be fresh or the customer will know it. Since the inside leaves from a head of lettuce curl up and won't lie flat in the sandwich, we couldn't use them, and that meant waste. Lettuce and tomato was a big issue for us. Because so many customers wanted it, I decided we had to offer both, but it wasn't an easy decision.

3. *It had to be customized.* We stressed we were M-A-D-E— T-O—O-R-D-E-R. We offered eight condiments—ketchup, mustard, pickle, lettuce, onion, tomato, mayonnaise, and relish. Cheese was optional. That gave the customer plenty of choices, but just how many? I didn't know how to figure it out, so I asked an Ohio State University accounting student who worked for us named Roger Webb to figure it out. When I asked him, Roger's eyes blinked like the lights on one of those old Univac computers, and I thought he said, "It's

simple, Dave, two to the Power of Ate." "Smart alec, this has nothing to do with how hearty their appetite is," I bounced back at him. "Just tell me how many choices the customer has!" "Dave, it's 256 choices, which is two to the power of the number eight. That's a logarithm."

Roger came to work for us full time and made plenty of other contributions. The 256 choices became a theme that drove our advertising program with lots of success, but, to this day, I still don't know what Roger was talking about. I have never ever seen a log that had any rhythm, and even if it did, what would that have to do with the number of choices on a menu?

4. *And, you had to have a nice place where you could eat it.* I wanted a building that had carpeting, and one where we didn't tell you to hurry up and get the heck out of there.

Wendy's was built with the idea of accommodating the customer at a time when the customer thought that the idea of service was history. We put out the message: We'll take care of you. And we do.

We weren't and aren't a fast-food restaurant. I hate the term "fast food," especially when it's applied to Wendy's. Our SERVICE is fast. Our goal is to get the order to the customer in fifteen seconds at the counter and thirty seconds at the Pick-Up window. Our food is not cooked any faster or slower than any other restaurant's. We don't cook by machine, and our restaurants don't look like they popped out of some plastic mold. Go into some of those places and you'd swear they clean the dining room with a water hose.

When I first started, we got 55 cents for a Wendy's single, which is a quarter-pound hamburger, and 75 cents with cheese, lettuce, and tomato. McDonald's sold its smaller hamburger for 15 cents until 1967, when it went to 18 cents. In 1969, McDonald's didn't yet have their quarter pounder. So,

McDonald's was offering an 18-cent deal against mine, which was three times the price. Experts said I'd never make it, but they were wrong because people want quality and they'll pay for it.

People have often asked me why we had chili on the menu from the start. It's real easy: What do you do with the leftover hamburger? The recipe was the hard part. I can still remember the marathon cooking sessions that we used to do between Charlotte Immke's kitchen (Len's wife) and Lorraine's kitchen at home. Our chili is meaty, and I think it's healthy. The beans are high in fiber and the chili is low in fat.

The first big change in the menu took place in 1979. Ground beef prices jumped from 72 cents a pound in 1978 to $1.40 in 1979. We had to raise our menu prices and that hurt our business. At about the same time, the first wave of nutrition concerns about beef came up, and more people were on diets and health kicks, too. It was the first time we had to do more than open up our doors and let people come in. By late 1979, our sales were down 17%.

Calories, saturated fats, and cholesterol were the bad guys, and bulk, fiber, and whole grains were the guys in the white hats. Although experts still don't agree on the effects of cholesterol and saturated fats, Americans still eat plenty of hamburgers when the craving hits, but soaring beef prices and the nutrition issue drove us to make the first big change. As with most of the changes we made, it was simply a question of keeping our antenna up to what was happening in the marketplace.

Many people don't realize it, but the whole business of fast food became a new ballgame when the baby boomers matured and consumers became more discriminating and health-conscious. In the fall of 1979 we introduced a fresh garden salad bar, the first new product we'd ever added to our menu. This new addition featured fourteen items and seven salad dressings and was an immediate hit with our customers, especially the women, who were entering the work force in unbelievable numbers at that time. We were the first national chain to go with a salad bar. So in 1980, sales took off because of the salad bar. This didn't hurt our expenses, either, since ground beef was continuing to go up in price and the supply was getting tighter. Remember those inner lettuce leaves we were wasting? The salad was the perfect solution. Because onions, tomatoes, and lettuce were already part of the morning prep-work program for each restaurant, the salad bar was a business natural for us.

In April of 1980, we added a chicken sandwich to attract those customers who wanted a sandwich other than a hamburger. We also added a Kids' Meal to increase our share of the family business.

More new products came in 1983. In November, we added more variety to the salad bar and started offering the hot stuffed baked potato. This strengthened our selection with people who were concerned with nutrition. Again, we were the first national chain to come out with a baked potato. In 1990, we came out with the skinless, grilled chicken sandwich—again thinking about the nutrition trend.

In 1989, we added the Super Value Menu, which was devised by George Condos, one of our senior vice presidents, and his people. This is a selection of seven items available for 99 cents in most restaurants. It includes a two-ounce Junior Bacon Cheeseburger, the garden salad, baked potato, chili, a "Biggie" fry, "Biggie" drink, and a Frosty. This concept is known as "bundling." Instead of running a different cents-off promotion every day, we "bundle" a whole menu of products you can buy for 99 cents each, every day. It sends the message that there is always a good value at Wendy's seven days a week.

Our Super Value program lets customers know that

Wendy's high quality doesn't have to mean high prices. Over the years, the rest of the industry (especially McDonald's and Burger King) have tried to move into our niche with larger, more expensive sandwiches. Like their other products, these new items were still prepackaged and not very good. Still, they were cutting into our business because they now had both the inexpensive items aimed largely at the kids' market along with larger, pricier numbers aimed at adults. Our strategy has been to maintain Wendy's high quality but to round our menu out with a few lower-priced products.

As a result, Wendy's combination of high-quality food and competitive prices makes it the first-choice, quick-service restaurant. We preach to our people about delivering total quality every day. But customers don't care about the preaching we do to our people or what I say in our commercials. After all, what do you go to a restaurant for? It's the eats. If you can't deliver, then it's a zero. If we tell people that Wendy's has the best food around, then it better be true. That's my way and our focus.

If you lose sight of the way and the focus, there's trouble—as we learned when we tried to get into the breakfast business. Breakfast is really hard to do, and we have never really done it right. We first started playing around with breakfast in 1979 and initially went at it whole hog—hash browns, biscuits, bacon. In 1983, we narrowed it down to omelets and breakfast sandwiches. Plenty of people like to eat our food while they're driving or riding in a car. You just can't do that with an omelet.

Then there are operating problems. You have to get up and get the people there. The breakfast market really isn't as good as it was because everybody's in it now, including the supermarket freezer case with breakfast sandwiches that you can pop in the microwave.

More than other quick-service restaurants, breakfast didn't

work with the rest of our business. It actually cannibalized the
rest of our day. You see, when somebody goes someplace for
breakfast, they are not likely to come back again that day.
The big breakfast is mostly eaten these days by your lumber-
jack or your heavyweight boxer. Today's breakfast is a
smaller ticket item, while lunch and dinner are a bigger ticket.
We have to protect that lunch and dinner business. We have
breakfast on freeway stops and downtown locations, where it
really works out.

Although breakfast is a softspot for us, dinner may be our
biggest opportunity yet. We also have an advantage with the
health and weight conscious adult. Working off the strength
of our salad bar, we expanded it in 1987 with the Wendy's
SuperBar, which added hot Italian and Mexican items to the
salad choices. We offer it both at lunch and dinner. Since the
SuperBar is self-service, food costs are slightly higher, but
labor costs are lower. That's a factor as the minimum wage
goes up, and more and more full-service restaurants are hurt
by climbing liquor prices (sin taxes) and lawsuits against customers who drink and then are involved in accidents.

Back in 1982, we tested a full dinner menu in Cincinnati
with items like chicken parmesan and ground beef in mush-
room sauce, but that's not our thing.

We've studied it and found that a family eats together in a
restaurant because it wants to, not because there are all kinds
of different items to eat. Family dinner, family values, good
family pricing. These frozen-food ads on TV that you see
where everybody has to have something completely different
are mostly hype.

What counts most about our menu is what customers say.
They say it in what they buy. They say it even better in the
letters I get. I'll tell you that the letter I got recently from Ms.
Erin Stralka convinced me that our menu choices are doing
the right thing by young families:

I like your cheese hamburgers. And I like your French fries and your frostys. My name is Erin Stralka. I am 7 yers old. We are starding to go to Wendys after Church instead of Mcdonalds.

Not only does Ms. Stralka have more guts than I had at the age of seven (I would never have dreamed of writing the Senior Chairman of the Board of anything when I was that young), but she also spells better, and since she did this on a personal computer, she is light-years ahead of me in technology. And her letter is telling me some very, very good news.

Dave's Rules on Giving Customers Choices

Any business—whether it's run by a certified accountant or a rocket scientist—offers a certain number of products. You either do personal tax returns or you don't. Your rockets can either launch satellites or they can't. The thought we put into designing the Wendy's menu can provide some guidelines on how a business should handle the range of products it offers and when it should change them. There may be something here for retailers, for manufacturers, and even for folks who run service businesses. Remember, the best way to serve the customer is not to offer the MOST CHOICES but THE MOST SENSIBLE CHOICES in whatever your pocket of strength is.

1. *Keep it focused.* You can't offer the customer a real choice unless you're organized. You can't be all over the map. First, you take a position that you're in the hamburger sandwich business, then you figure out the key kinds of hamburgers you have to offer to be in that business, and have what most people want. You can't jump from one thing to another

and add Reuben sandwiches one day and stuffed pita bread the next. It confuses the customer, and there's no way that you can deliver consistent quality in everything you make if you keep jumping around.

2. *Watch for creep.* When I took over the Columbus Kentucky Fried Chicken operation, there were a hundred items on the menu! That didn't happen overnight, just like people don't load up their attic overnight. If you add an item, ask yourself: What am I going to get rid of to make room for it?

3. *Manage your in-and-out items tight.* We have in-and-out items that are on the menu for a limited time. They create excitement. The Dave's Deluxe hamburger is an item like that, and it's a good sandwich. When we promote it on national television, we can't make them fast enough. Without TV exposure, we don't sell very many. That means it should come off the menu. If it stays on without the promotion, it just takes away from your focus, and it isn't special anymore. You've seen shops that have been running "going out of business" sales for two years. Nobody believes you. Any special offer is like that.

4. *Keep checking to make sure the customer understands who you are.* Every month, we are out there asking five hundred people what they think Wendy's is and how they think we are doing. Most people think we're the best place for hamburgers, chicken sandwiches, and salads. When hamburger chains add things like pizza to their menu, I think that they have walked over the edge. People don't know what you are anymore.

5. *Take each key item or group of items you offer and look at the whole picture.* We used to have a hundred people in Wendy's marketing department. They would sit around saying let's do this or let's do that, and we ended up doing nothing. Now, we have thirty-nine people and each person is

focused on getting something done. We have one person in charge of chili. Another is responsible for baked potatoes, another for grilled chicken, and so forth. Mr. Baked Potato thinks about baked potatoes as a main course . . . and as a side order . . . and as a snack. He looks at how often the baked potato is mentioned in our ads or how much it's on our tray liners. He's responsible for looking at baked potatoes from all the angles. Instead of having a hundred people looking at Wendy's marketing in general, we have fewer people—each focused on our products one by one.

6. *Check the trends.* When you look at how Wendy's menu has changed, very few of the changes were brainstorms we just dreamed up. They were answers to questions like: How do we give customers more nutritious choices? Since chicken is more popular, what is the right kind of chicken sandwich for us? If people want salads, how do we give them a fresh salad bar? These were all trends coming from new ways people were living, new life-styles. You learn the trends from the TV, from magazines, from walking down the street, or watching how people behave in shopping malls. You learn the trends by sniffing around.

Competing the Wendy's Way

Many of you will remember when you were in grade school kids used to get into real fights about brands. You know, "Our Motorola TV is better than your Zenith," and stuff like that. Those kinds of spats are history. Brands used to be part of people's dreams. Years ago, it was: "My dad drove a Chevy, I'm going to drive a Chevy." Or: "My Mom washes her clothes in a Kenmore. Honey, can we have a Kenmore washer when we get married?" Today, people want and expect a choice. Brands are just not that important to people.

There are many more brands today, and the differences between most of them have become smaller and smaller.

Because the world is different, you can't compete the same way you used to. First, you don't win customers over for life. In the restaurant business, you have to win them every visit. Second, a business like Wendy's takes plenty of fine-tuning. And you can't fine-tune something that's as delicate as an electronic ignition with a monkey wrench. Overreact to what competition does and you could stand the company on its head in a matter of hours. Third, it's dumber and dumber to try to bluff and fake out competitors. Customers don't care if we outfox McDonald's or outsmart Burger King. All they want to know is where they can depend on getting the best sandwich or salad at the right price. We call that "price-value."

Wendy's competes differently, but I think that we're the new wave of competition. Ray Kroc, the guy who made McDonald's, was once asked what he would do if he found out one of his competitors was drowning. " 'Put a hose in his mouth,' "[5] was his answer. Our take on competition boils down to one principle: We compete by focusing on our customer rather than on our competition. I've got a few other tips on competing. For whatever they're worth, here they are.

How to Win
Without Jabbing People in the Eyeballs

1. *Give your customers fewer problems.* In the early days at our first restaurant, I used to watch people who worked for us. I knew it would be easy to get complacent because things

---

[5] *The Economist* magazine, February 17, 1990.

were working well. I came to the conclusion that laziness and complacency cause trouble. So I decided we needed more "problems" if we were to create fewer problems for our customers and give them more reasons to come to Wendy's. I began to insist on certain things being done with more care and precision and got fanatical about cleanliness. We taught our employees that Wendy's business goal was to make sure customers had problem-free experiences when they came to our restaurants. We made this a merchandising campaign and our operating creed. I guess it's summed up best as "Doing It Dave's Way."

2. *Next, look straight ahead.* I'm often asked, "What should one of our restaurant managers focus on when they look at competition?" That's about the dumbest thing he can do. Instead, he should focus on what he is doing, and concentrate on giving the best service in the cleanest restaurant instead of worrying about the guy across the street. People at the district and regional levels worry about the trends and the competition. We want the restaurant manager focused inward. A manager shouldn't be worried about marketing, but he should know when to call for some marketing support around his restaurant. A good manager will promote the business within the community and be active in civic affairs. But we don't want him so involved that you can't find him when there's a problem in the restaurant.

If a competitor is full and we're empty, we want to know why he is doing so much business, but the answer to that is likely to be our own problems rather than something fantastic that the competitor is doing. We can be our own worst competition, and we can hurt ourselves awful bad. I love competition that worries about us more than they worry about themselves, because this is an execution business pure and simple. Back when I was with Kentucky Fried Chicken, there was a competitor who ran a restaurant across the street from one of ours. He used to sit in his car outside of my place every day instead of running his own business. He would watch everything we were doing. Can you guess which business slowly went down the tubes?

3. *Don't bounce your resources around.* When we fooled around with the breakfast business a few years ago, we pulled dollars and people away from promoting our hamburgers, chicken, and salads. That hurt us. You have to remind the customer every day where you are strong. You can't launch a new business just because everybody else has gotten into it, unless you can really afford a whole lot of extra expense and people.

4. *Make the right impression on the customer.* We have really clean, sharp-looking offices at our headquarters in Dublin, Ohio. That's nice, but it's more important that our restaurants be clean and sharp. But if we were in the business of running medical clinics, let's say, how our office looked would be critical. It wouldn't have to be fancy, but it would need to be neat and clean. You could be visiting the best heart surgeon in the world, and you'd have second thoughts about letting him tinker with you if you walked into his office and saw instruments on the floor or smudges all over the X-ray machine.

Look at every part of your business, every part of the impression you make on the customer. A couple of years ago our restaurant facilities were flat-out noncompetitive. We hadn't reinvested in remodeling as we should have. They were real tired. They were dark. The old newsprint surfaces still decorated the counters and tabletops. The look was dated. The restrooms didn't match the Wendy's expectations. We spent $18 million in 1989 to lighten up and brighten up the restaurants. That's not maintenance. We put greenhouses on most company restaurants. We created the impression that people expected from a quality restaurant.

5. *Behave yourself.* I could give a guy like Jim Near, Wendy's CEO, a Wendy's anywhere. It could be in the boondocks or in the toughest slum in the worst city you could pick. In six months, people within a three-mile radius of that restaurant would know: (1) that Jim Near has a Wendy's at the corner of X and Y; (2) the food is terrific; (3) the service—unbelievable; and (4) the restaurant—clean. He will make money, because HE WILL GO IN THERE AND BEHAVE HIMSELF. Behaving yourself simply means staying focused and doing the basic things day after day to keep your customers, your employees, your suppliers, and your neighbors in the community satisfied. Follow the play book and keep the right attitude. To win in our business, we just have to behave ourselves, seven days a week.

We want the customer to think a minute before he stops in a competitor's parking lot or before he opens a competitor's doors. We want him to ask himself, "Are they really going to give me what I want the way Wendy's will?"

Some companies compete by trying to outmaneuver their rivals. At Wendy's, we do it by paying attention to the customer and then paying attention to ourselves so that we are as good as the customer expects us to be.

8

The Secret Code to Wendy's Success

What exactly makes Wendy's different? I've told you about how we make a different kind of product from our competitors. We also have a different setup, a different system from other people in the quick-service business. I'm not talking about computer systems. It's the operating systems I mean. People take them for granted, but I want you to hear more about them. Our systems are really as important to Wendy's success as anything on our menu or our commitment to quality operations. The value of these systems has been learned or proven in some true-to-life cases that have been both fun and a challenge to solve. Let me tell you about them.

The Story Behind the Snake

When I looked at the "fast feeders" expanding in the sixties, they reminded me more and more of the grocery store. What was it about them that gave them that grocery-store feel? One day, I put my finger on it: It was the way people lined up to be waited on! It really said to the customer: self-service, just like at the cash registers in the grocery store or the discount house. Serve yourself, buddy, because we sure aren't going to serve you. Another thing about lining up grocery-store style: It's the scramble system. If you're like me, you always get in the wrong line, and you're stuck there tapping your toes. Or if a new register opens up, everybody dives for it like it was the last life raft on the *Titanic!* The whole program does not bring out warm feelings in people. When folks come into Wendy's, we want them to enjoy their food . . . not practice the law of the jungle.

To create the right atmosphere, one person should be taking the orders, and that person should be really skilled in taking orders and dealing with people. The order taker at Wendy's is a key player who helps set the mood of the entire restaurant. Our system is consciously set up to affect, and we hope improve, the customer's mood more than other quick-service restaurants. In those few seconds that it takes for the order to come up, the order taker can make a little quick conversation, especially if he or she knows the customer. So, we become a more personable place.

If one person's taking the orders, then it made sense that all the people coming into the restaurant would line up in a single line. But, with the number of people in our restaurants at rush hour, that would be a pretty long line. So, we set up cordons that let us push the line together, that let it zigzag. And, the snake was born.

When things get really busy, we send another order taker down the line to help get the orders in fast. And, since we specialized the order-taking job, we could handle preparing and packaging the food with fewer people and do it in less time. Most Wendy's, except for some on freeways, where people are totally pressed for time, have a single customer line. As long as that line moves along, people are happy. As you can guess, keeping that line moving is our number one job.

All this spins off one word: FRESH. If you want it fresh and you want it fast, I think this is the only way you can organize a chain of four thousand restaurants to do it. But that means our people are on the firing line all the time. Serving the customer at a Wendy's is more complicated than at some of our rivals. Workers will come to us from other competitors and discover that you really have to work here. But there is much higher self-satisfaction for our employees than in many of the other chains.

Riding the Wave

Gordon Teter—our president and chief operating officer—is about as bright as they come. Sometimes when he talks to me I've got to say, "Gordon, slow down and go back. You've left me at the last station."

One day, I was telling Gordon—who had joined us from Ponderosa Steak House—about how Phil Clauss had hired the Chicago consultant back at the Hobby House and how we decided that the real answer to our slack times in the afternoon wasn't one the consultant recommended, but rather getting on our feet and doing things—wiping windows and keeping busy.

Gordon's eyes lit up and he nodded: "You mean THE WAVE."

I said, "THE WHAT?"

Again, he said "the wave," and then he went on to explain his version of it.

Business moves through a restaurant in waves. A bad manager will be behind the wave, picking up the clutter, always trying to catch up. The manager who's on top of things will always be ready for customers, ahead of the wave all the way.

You can tell as much about a restaurant during the "down" time as during the peak time. After the rush, you have to clean the doors and empty the trash bins. When you go into a restaurant after the rush and no one is doing cleanup, you can pretty much tell that it's a low-volume, poorly managed unit.

If you learn to ride the wave well, the restaurant always has a quiet hum, always busy but never frantic. It never works too far ahead, and it never lets itself get behind. That's one reason you don't notice the crew and the management team nearly as much. We train them to be friendly and courteous, but they are also less visible. They're not in the way when you don't need them, so it feels more like a restaurant and less like a production line.

Well, I'm all for the wave now—now that I know what it means. As for Gordon, he's not nearly the computer that I make him out to be, but I'm sure glad his brains are on our side and not anybody else's.

The Case of the Sputtering Speaker

Two years after we launched Wendy's, Bob Barney came over to work for me as president of the company, and the first assignment I gave him was, "Make the drive-through window work." This was July 1971.

We knew that if we could offer a custom-made sandwich at a drive-through window, that would give us a real edge, but the program wasn't working. For some reason, the drive-through wasn't delivering the business we expected. The window accounted for only about 10% of our business. It didn't make sense. We had a separate cooking center for the drive-in, the employees in the restaurants knew we thought this business was important, and we had all the standard equipment like speakers in the drive-through line to take people's orders. What was the problem? And why weren't we able to figure it out?

Bob, who had been with Kentucky Fried Chicken and Arthur Treacher's earlier, told me that he had to learn the business from the ground up if he was going to solve the problem. So, he went to work on the restaurant floor and looked at the window from the INSIDE, from the viewpoint of everything else going on in the restaurant. "Give me a few months and I'll have it working for you," he promised. I crossed my fingers.

The first thing Bob noticed was that we had created a whole new job in the restaurant, and that job was called "runner." The runner would jockey between the restaurant and the car lineup carrying in the orders. But, why did we have a runner in the first place? We were a drive-through, not a drive-in. Didn't we have a microphone and speaker system to take people's orders? Of course we did, but it didn't work any better than the microphone/speakers in all those drive-in restaurants back then. The equipment was dependable less than 50% of the time. The signal would break up, and the connections were worse than a short-wave radio. Instead of Clara Peller hollering, "Where's the Beef?" we had customers shouting, "Where's my order?" and frustrated order takers inside yelling back, "What did you say?" So, the problem of sales at the drive-through really turned out to be a communications problem. Bob junked the microphone/speakers we started with and installed some really fine equipment. This was just when real breakthroughs were being made in transistor electronics, so we were at the cutting edge. No more runners. The customer had to use the speaker system; and since the speaker now worked, this wasn't a problem anymore.

Not only did we put the equipment in, but we put it in a special place. We learned that if you had your speaker back far enough you could have about three different orders on the grill at the same time, and they would be put together like an assembly line. This was during a peak period when cars were lining up outside. Since we are selling a custom-made, not a prepackaged product, that gave us just the timing edge we needed to serve it both fresh and fast. With the communications straightened out and the pacing system down, the window grill that had been sitting in the corner unused started to cook. I mean really cook! It wasn't long before the window was doing 40% of the business.

We also officially changed the name to Pick-Up Window from drive-in, because drive-ins had a bad name as hangouts for cruisers and joy-riders. The basic Pick-Up Window principles are still the same today. They still work, though you will now see employees working the Pick-Up station with "Walkman"-style headsets with microphones, through which they communicate with the customer. This lets them move around easier and gives us even better communication with the customer.

Bob Barney retired in 1989, but the Pick-Up Window is where he made a lasting impact on Wendy's. Today, we have the best Pick-Up Window in the business. The target time to fill an order from the time it's placed until the time it's in the customer's hands is thirty seconds. The window accounts for 40–45% of our sales. And that's not all. Perfecting the window has had a terrific bearing on another very expensive cost: real estate. When a high percentage of your business goes through the drive-through window, you're able to reduce the size of the parking lots. Perfecting the drive-through helped everybody in our business save money on real estate.

The Case of the Grudging Griller

In 1985, I was visiting some stores in Wisconsin, and at one I saw an unusually long line at lunch time. We like plenty of customers, but that long line did not make me happy. A long line does not necessarily mean that you are doing a terrific business. It usually means that you are doing something wrong. I have always preached that you can do as much business as you want to do if you can keep your lines the shortest. If customers see a long line they may leave, and customers driving down the street won't even pull in if they see a long line. So restaurants with the shortest lines will get the most business during busy periods.

When I went inside, the long line at the Pick-Up Window was matched by a backed-up line inside. I found the manager and told him I wanted to talk. He headed for one of the dining room tables and stopped along the way to introduce me to the crew.

Now, I could see that the line was getting even longer because the help was paying attention to me and not to the customers. I told the manager to hold off. "Go behind the counter and get through your lunch rush and then we'll meet and talk," I said.

Now, there are two grill areas in every restaurant, and the reason for the second (the window grill) is to make drive-through a separate business in order to speed up service, just like Bob Barney laid it out back in the early seventies. I went behind the counter myself and noticed that the Pick-Up Window grill wasn't turned on. Mystery solved. I knew then why the lines were so long. They were using only one grill to service both the front and the window, and they couldn't get the product out fast enough.

After lunch, I asked the manager why. He complained that sales were off and they didn't need two grills going. He was ruining his business and our reputation because he grudged paying the utilities to run the second grill. But, I wanted to step through the whole list in hopes that the manager would figure out what he was doing wrong himself.

"Why are sales off? Are you paying attention to quality?" I asked.

"Yes, that's not our problem," he said.

"Is it couponing from competition?"

"No, that's not our problem," he repeated.

Finally, I asked him again, "Why is your Pick-Up grill turned off?"

"We don't do enough business to put it on," he said. "I've already told you that!"

"Don't you think that if you turned it on you'd be able to do more business?"

"You just don't understand, Mr. Thomas," he said. "It's only like this for twenty or thirty minutes right at lunchtime."

The manager didn't even understand the very peaks that are the heart of our business. I was fuming. I hate to see slow service and can't stand to see customers waiting. I held my temper and waited until we got back to the hotel room. The manager was there, the owner of the restaurant for whom the manager worked, along with a couple of us from Columbus. We were relaxed and sipping soft drinks.

I brought up the pick-up grill again. The owner gave me the same answer as the manager did, and I didn't accept it from him, either. "You don't run your business to lose money, do you?" I asked.

"Of course not, Mr. Thomas, that's silly," the owner responded.

"You bought a Wendy's franchise so all the key questions would be answered, so all the problems would be solved for you," I said. "You can't run a successful business if you don't pay attention to the things we have created in the Wendy's concept. You've got a Pick-Up Window grill, turn it on. That's why it's there."

The owner was polite, but I could tell he was really disgusted with me and couldn't wait to get out of that hotel room. I hit the problem one more time before he got away. "Try it at lunchtime only and build it from there. I promise you'll get your sales back up. Try it."

One month later, I got a telephone message. "Tell Dave Thomas that he was right." Two days later I got a letter from the owner. "Thank you for kicking me in the ass. That's exactly what I needed. I kept looking around for excuses and couldn't see the problem which was right in front of my eyes. I was madder than hell when you left, but we're seeing a slow build of our sales."

When you've got a concept that works, stick with it. Don't try to change it unless you have given it a lot of thought and come up with a better way, that, after being tested thoroughly, works.

Although I don't call it by that name, I tell the Case of the Grudging Griller often, and different people have gotten different things out of it. Here are some of the other lessons managers have learned from it:

- Be careful how you pick the problems you THINK you need to solve. You can pay a big price for focusing on the wrong problem.
- Watch out for chances to save on expenses. Some of them will "save" you right into bankruptcy.
- Some employees will see your busiest and most important time as a nuisance, often because they're lazy. I think that was the case with this manager. He just wanted to get through this thirty minutes of hell during lunchtime, and

then things would be back to "normal." I always watch people to see if they gear up for business peaks or are intimidated by them.

- Look for the cloud behind the silver lining. The long lines inside and outside the restaurant should have been telling the owner and manager something. That something was not that they were that great but that they weren't serving the customer. In the same way, companies that have a big backlog of orders or lots of requests for work they can't fill are sure to run into trouble sooner or later. Somebody else will just slice off the extra business, often by making a carbon copy of the first company.

The Case of the Telltale Crackle

"Slacking the fries" means defrosting the french fries to the right temperature before you cook them. You tell a restaurant manager that he's not slacking his fries properly, and that's a real insult. It's like saying something very unkind about their spouse.

Ed Ourant is a big guy—Sly Stallone-size, but definitely better-looking. And, Ed—since he's one of our top operations guys—has really keen senses. He has a terrific nose, but what really amazes me about Ed are his ears. He has ears like a piano tuner.

One day, Ed and I walked into a restaurant in West Virginia, and he told the manager the instant he walked in the door: "Gary, you're not slacking your fries." Well, Gary—all 6 foot 6 of him—turned five shades of red and nearly invited Ed to go out to the parking lot and settle this thing man to man. But, all of us, being good diplomats, moved to a table, and Gary went to get us something to eat, and I was sure he was also going to prove to himself that his fries were being slacked exactly according to procedure.

About two minutes later, Gary comes back with our order and his tail between his legs like a beaten puppy. "Ed," he said, his eyes looking at the floor, "you were right, the fries weren't being slacked. BUT HOW DID YOU KNOW? Have you got spies in my kitchen? Who called ahead and told you?"

Ed explained that he didn't need spies. When he came in the door, he could hear this little background noise of crackling and popping. It comes from the water and ice on the fries hitting the hot oil. Properly slacked fries slide into the oil like silk down a silver chute. You don't hear a sound, and the fry that cooks up is much better-tasting.

The lesson here is that people are trained to inspect a business with their eyes, but a really strong system challenges its people to use all of their senses all the time to check up on things. Taste, touch, hearing, and smell. All count. I'll tell you about smell in just a second.

9

Salad Bars Won't Do Windows

At our 1980 franchisee convention, speaker after speaker raved about the success of our new salad bar. We saw graphs, sales charts, and results of customer surveys. Everybody went on and on praising the salad bar as the savior of Wendy's. Because we introduced a salad bar customers would once again beat a path to our door.

When everyone was finished speaking, I stood up. "Here's the only thing I want you to remember about my talk tonight: The salad bar won't wash your windows!"

Everybody laughed, but I was serious. I went on to explain what I meant: "If you think the salad bar is going to keep your windows clean or your parking lot clean or is going to change the fact that you have to remind your people to smile at customers, then you are absolutely wrong. You cannot forget the basics of this business. The salad bar is not infallible. It's a product. It's not Midas turning everything to gold. It doesn't run itself. Times change, and customer tastes change, that's true, and we have to do new things that will help. But if you stray from the basics of your business, you're in trouble."

In the case of Wendy's, basics means operations. It's the heart of our business.

If you want to be a strong operator, you better love repetition. I've seen MBAs who are learning the business. They mop the floor once and say, "O.K., what's next?" They *think* they know what mopping the floor means, but they don't. They don't understand the repetition. It's not doing it once, but understanding that it must be done constantly . . . and that you must have people in the restaurants who want to do it constantly. You have to want to reach for the dust in the corners. People think we're a marketing company, but we really aren't. We're an operations company.

The first thing I notice when I walk into a Wendy's is the smell. I can tell as I walk through the door if the crew has been doing the floors with a sour mop—a mop that's not been properly cleaned. Thank God it doesn't happen often. One day, I got so furious when that smell hit me, I said to the manager, "Mister, you've invented a totally new way to clean a restaurant . . . with a dirty mop. That's one heck of a breakthrough. Are you going to franchise it, Einstein?" I was hopping mad. When it comes to cleanliness, I get serious real fast.

A restaurant manager has over sixty things to watch over while he's running the ship. Customers have just one thing to do, so they have plenty of time to watch what we don't do. That's the way I look at it.

When I go to a Wendy's, I look at a restaurant the same way that you do. The first thing I'll do is look at the food. I sneak a peek at what's on other people's plates. Is that a good-looking chicken sandwich? Are those french fries golden brown? Is the cashier smiling and asking, "Can we help you?" Do you feel that the folks behind the counter are really glad you came in? Did I get what I ordered and did it taste good? Is the place clean? If all these things are right and you feel that you made the right decision coming to Wendy's, then we have what I call a "WOW" restaurant. In fact, I think customers are so smart that they have a checklist in their head that they use to grade their experience in the restaurant.

I'll share that checklist with you, even though I think it's our secret weapon. Our ability to get this checklist right is more important than our chili recipe or how we make our Frosties. There are plenty of other chains who think they understand the customer's checklist, too. But, I don't think that there is anyone who takes it as seriously as we do.

The Wendy's Customer Checklist

Service:

- Were you greeted properly by the person who took your order? Our order taker is a really important person. He or she has to have plenty of self-confidence and motivation. They set the mood and the pace.
- Was your order served promptly? (We have specific time goals for service, and we constantly monitor the restaurants to ensure they're met.)
- Did you get what you asked for?
- If there was a problem, was it handled properly?

People:

- Did the employees in the restaurant have a friendly and courteous attitude? Were they neat and clean and wearing their uniforms properly?
- Were there enough people on duty to serve the customers?
- Did they communicate easily, and were they well trained?

You can tell if a restaurant is excited about having customers come in. You can also read the enthusiasm on the customers' faces. A restaurant team that is disciplined and upbeat has a real effect on the customers. Not only are the customers happier, but it pays off in the business: If the customers are motivated, you will see it in the sales.

Food Quality:

- Did the food look and taste good?
- Was it served at the right temperature?
- Were they out of anything on the menu? Were any items missing from the salad bar that were supposed to be there?

Inside:

- Were the windows, counters, and floors clean?
- How about the restrooms? Were they clean? Did everything work? Was there plenty of paper and soap?
- Was the salad bar and condiment stand well stocked and neat?
- Were there enough tables and chairs? Were they clean, or dirty and littered?
- Was the look of the restaurant comfortable and pleasant?
- Was the dining room temperature right?
- Were the trash containers clean and not overfilled?

Outside:

- In the drive-through, how well does the speaker work? (If it's raining, I don't want a ten-minute conversation.)
- Is the parking lot trashed up? Are there potholes in it? Are the trash containers clean?
- What about the little things like the phone booth? (Is it working?) Newspaper stand. (Is it stocked?)

This checklist is merely a first step. It's doing something about it that makes the difference between a great restaurant and one that's mediocre.

Our attention to detail pays off. Opinions on 90% of the comment cards filled out by customers are positive. That is really high. Even the negative comments we get are nicely worded. "We enjoyed eating at your restaurant, but we think you could improve . . ." The biggest concern customers will have is whether they got what they ordered. This is something we have to work on every day. Since every sandwich at Wendy's is custom-made, there's a greater risk of making mistakes. We'll never get it perfect, but we'll try really hard for every customer order.

We take the customer's mental checklist very seriously, so seriously in fact that we have turned it into a checklist form that our district and headquarters managers use to check out a store when they make a visit. We have also built a program around this form and the discipline it requires. We call the whole program SPARKLE. Next to the food, SPARKLE is the hottest thing in Wendy's. Let me tell you how it works.

SPARKLE is an ongoing inspection of quality, service, and cleanliness in Wendy's restaurants. We have turned serving the customer right into a continuous contest between our four thousand restaurants. SPARKLE "inspectors," who include top managers from throughout the company, visit each location constantly. We're not talking about an annual visit where the regional manager comes in and gabs with the restaurant manager over a cup of coffee for half an hour. Every Wendy's restaurant is evaluated on unannounced visits, at least eight to twelve times a year!

Each inspector, who is also really a judge for the contest, too, comes at it from a little different, and hopefully a little tougher, perspective than an individual customer would. We look at the corners harder. We're tougher on service times, order accuracy, and customer service. And cleanliness is tops on our list: How much flying food and smashed cracker is left from the little guy who last sat on that booster chair? It better be none. This impression really impacts the mother: That booster chair has to be clean, and it has to be in the right place for her to find it.

We also look at consistency. One day you'll get great food and service. The next day, the food may be great but the service will be off. The drive-through will work one day. The next day, the order will have the wrong condiments. We will actually evaluate stores numerous times for consistency.

The SPARKLE program got dreamed up the same way so many other things happen at Wendy's. I had a gnawing idea that we needed to do something to improve the discipline in our restaurant on basic things. When I talked it over with Ed Ourant, Ed said, "I know just what you mean . . . you want the stores to SPARKLE, don't you?" "Yeah! Yeah! You got it," I was yelling. I was so excited that I stampeded out into the hallway outside of my office looking for my secretary to get the idea written down. As I was walking out, I bumped into Gilles Gallant, our senior vice president based in Chicago. Poor Gilles—I learned later—was on his way to the men's room. Well, I lassoed him and brought him into the office. Twenty minutes later, Gilles had given us a rough plan of how he would do a program that would make our restaurants sparkle. The meeting happened in February. By September, we were picking the first winners in the contest. I'll never forget the look of relief that Gilles had on his face when the first meeting broke up and he dashed for the hallway. Dummy me, I thought it was all because we had fixed a big operating problem for him!

A young guy by the name of Mike Watson is now in charge of the SPARKLE program. He's earned the name Mr. Sparkle, and does he know how to keep people fired up. We have run the SPARKLE program for three years so far, but I expect it to be around a long time. We start with four thousand restaurants worldwide and then we cull our list down to the top four to five hundred restaurants. They then compete to reduce the list to one hundred units. Finally, we establish the top store in each of our eight regions. For the final competition, there are four judges, and I'm one of them. Fourteen-hour days and thirty thousand miles of travel are expected of the judges in the last round.

What's in it for the employees? In SPARKLE, we teach them how to run excellent restaurants. Then we recognize the top performers with cash and prizes. The top four hundred general managers get cash awards, and the eight regional finalists get $5,000. The top SPARKLE restaurant manager gets cash and a new car! We also have cash incentives at the local level. We spend over a million dollars each year to make our restaurants SPARKLE.

You remember in school how you could pretty much tell an A student from a B student from a C student . . . and you could always tell an F student. Well, in addition to the checklist, we also have a mental picture of what an A restaurant looks like and a B restaurant . . . and so forth. We have some C and F restaurants, but not too many and not for long.

George Condos, our Senior Vice-President of the Southwest region who, with his people, dreamed up the Super Value Menu I talked about earlier, came up with these descriptions of the different levels of restaurant performance, and I think that they're pretty good.

An F restaurant could have slow service, be indifferent to customers, or not be as clean as it should be. The food quality could be off or the customers' orders not accurate. Just one of these problems is enough for a restaurant to be an F, a failure, if a customer is offended. In an F restaurant, customers are there because of convenience, not because of choice. We worry a lot whenever we find an F restaurant, and we move in fast. First, because of what it is not doing for the customers it has. Second, because an F restaurant can do big damage to the Wendy's name.

A C restaurant is, well, average. It is as good as the competition, but not any better. Sometimes, there are problems getting consistency: The restaurant seems to work better, let's say, on Tuesday afternoon than on Thursday night. If that happens, it's almost sure that there are different managers on duty, and they have different standards for what they expect. Customers will have both positive and negative experiences. That means there is less repeat business. The C restaurant's share of the market is falling off, sometimes very slowly, in little bits and pieces. And, when the competition puts out a flood of coupons or offers Ninja Turtle dolls, a C restaurant's business fizzles. Like a C student, when the teacher pulls a surprise quiz, things can get dicey.

The B restaurant, on the other hand, does its job well and is a very solid performer. It will get very few negative comments, but customers will not be blown away by the positives, either. A customer will drive past the competition to get to us—IF the competition has operating problems. A B restaurant may hold its share of the market, but it is unlikely to gain share, just like a B student isn't likely to win any scholarships.

An A restaurant is a great operation. Guests are very pleased and impressed by courtesy, food, speed, and quality. It's a restaurant customers tell their friends about. It gets plenty of word-of-mouth advertising. Customers drive past the competition to get there, just like college recruiters go out of their way to sign up the best students. An A restaurant is taking away share from its competitors. When competitors do big give-aways, you will hardly notice any drop-off in an A restaurant's sales.

Take these descriptions, and substitute "dry cleaner," "jewelry store," "car wash," or any other service business for "restaurant" . . . and I think the same principle holds up. This is a very simple and dependable way, I think, to rank any kind of service business. Because it's simple and clear, it really works in a chain of four thousand separate businesses. How do we know that SPARKLE works? Nearly all of the top one hundred restaurants certified in the SPARKLE program do about $1 million annually in sales, or have registered double-digit sales increases over the preceding year.

SPARKLE may sound as regimented as a precision drill in the Marines. But, it's not that way. The eight SPARKLE restaurants we choose each year all have super high standards, but each has a unique personality, too. If you think about it, that's the way it should be, and that's for two reasons. First, a restaurant is really a team made up of people. So, it will have its own style, just like the Cincinnati Reds and the San Francisco Forty-Niners do. Second, any strong team will show the traits of its manager. That manager will walk on burning coals to keep the team motivated and focused on the right issues.

Take Debbie Tanner, who runs the Tualatin Wendy's restaurant outside of Portland, Oregon. Debbie is a fanatic about training, and she's an ace communicator. But, she also knows how important it is to make the job fun. "We have a good time here," she told me.

Remember I said that Wendy's didn't have a company song? Another SPARKLE winner, Dana Pontiff in Houston, has a crew member who actually came up with a song, well, about our Dave's Deluxe sandwich. They rang a bell, too, as an incentive for the crew when they sold a Dave's Deluxe, and the customers loved it, she says. Good thing I wasn't there when they did it, though. All this racket over a sandwich with my name on it would be a little embarrassing.

Dana's team has crew breakfasts. They've had a barbecue. They play baseball and go swimming. They do things as a group. What does it remind you of? "It's just like a family," Dana says. There you have the secret. Here's the manager of one of the eight best-managed restaurants in what I think is the best-run restaurant chain in the world, and what makes it all work for her? She thinks about her business as a family.

It's the same story for Patti Holmes, who runs the Monroeville Wendy's outside of Pittsburgh. Patti is also a SPARKLE champion. She says: "There is no such thing in Monroeville as overtraining. When we bring a new crew member into Monroeville, they are immediately part of the family, and everyone buys into training that individual." It sounds like the business version of a successful adoption to me.

Mert Onur manages our Wendy's restaurant in the Kadikoy District of Istanbul, Turkey. He's also our SPARKLE international grand prize winner. It's probably the most beautiful Wendy's in the world, and certainly one of the cleanest. Whenever I visit it, I feel like I'm visiting a family, not a restaurant.

Rap Sheet on a Real Operator

You'll never see Jim Near's face on the wall of the post office, but he's gotta be the shrewdest operator I know. He's also one of the finest and most honest people I've ever met.

I said that Wendy's is the best-run restaurant chain in the world. You also have to know that I don't run Wendy's day-to-day business. Jim Near is the chairman, CEO, and boss of operations. He's successful because he's a great operator. In fact, my business card says I'm Jim Near's "right-hand man."

If operations are so all-fired important, what is it that goes into a good operator? I noodled on that for a long time and decided that the best way to tell you about what goes into a real operator is to describe Jim Near, and to try to pick out the key traits in Jim's background that make him so terrific in the job he does.

Jim's father was in the restaurant business. Jim started out as a set-up boy in a drive-in in Columbus and really loved that place. He was into the business at an early age.

M.O. #1: Good operators like the business they're in, and often their parents were in it, too. That's especially true in restaurants.

Jim's employer took him from set-up boy to sandwich maker to fry boy. In 1954, a drive-in was a brand new concept. He learned all the positions that went into a drive-in. The business grew by leaps and bounds. He couldn't wait until school was out so he could get back to work. If he was lucky, he tells me, they'd let him work a double shift on Saturdays and Sundays.

M.O. #2: Good operators like to work hard. They like a fast pace, and they like to feel their adrenaline pump. I'm the same way except I pump my adrenaline a little slower now. As I say about exercise these days, the best thing I like about it is when it's over.

When he graduated from high school in 1956, the owners offered Jim the chance to become night manager of this drive-in for an impressive $125 a week. It was a tough decision, but his father insisted that he go to college instead. During the summers, he worked at the drive-in. At college, all of his papers were about the drive-in business.

M.O. #3: Smart operators today get an education—the best they can. Old-style operations used to be a combination of attention to detail, stamina, and gut instinct. Today, you have to understand systems and reports, too.

When he graduated from college, Jim went to Fort Knox as a National Guardsman. His former boss woke him up in his barracks in the middle of the night and asked if he had a job in mind when he was done with Basic. They wanted to start a chain of quick-service restaurants, featuring 15-cent hamburgers. This was going to be an early competitor against McDonald's, which was then poised to enter Columbus. "We gotta get ready for these guys," they said. They wanted him to be the general manager of this restaurant. They opened their first Burger Boy restaurant in 1961. By 1969, they had built fifty of these restaurants and sold them to the Borden company (you remember Elsie) for $10.5 million. Jim made a million dollars out of the deal.

M.O. #4: Good operators often make it big when they're pretty young. Usually they know the business so well, they have a good eye for growth concepts that will work. Also, since they're not a part of a big corporation, they move up faster.

Jim went with the deal to Borden. During the next four years, he reported into New York and learned a lot about corporate life. They treated him well and promoted him three times until he was president of Retail Sales in 1974. Over time, though, he got tired of the job, even though the Borden people were real nice to him. He was spending his time trying to keep people over him happy rather than running his business. So, he decided to leave Borden.

M.O. #5: Good operators are rarely happy pushing pencils or playing politics. They're too antsy. They'd rather get out and do something.

Jim studied Wendy's from the time we opened our first place down on Broad Street in Columbus. Soon, he got the Wendy's franchise for the entire state of West Virginia. Between '74 and '78, he built more Wendy's than any single franchisee: thirty-nine open and operating in the state and five more in Florida. He also opened seventeen Long John Silver seafood restaurants in Columbus. He grew well because he had the managers. He knew that the managers are always more critical to growth than the concept.

M.O. #6: The best operators know how to step on the gas when a concept is hot and bring it up to potential before competitors move in . . . but only if the business has the management strength it needs to grow fast.

Jim loves to study competition. Up until a couple years ago, if he saw a unique product on the menu, he would look for a way to walk through that kitchen and watch the cook make it. He'd ask to use the phone. Back then, phones almost always used to be in the kitchen. The restaurant workers just assumed he was from headquarters, but they forgot to ask which one.

Jim wants to know everything about how it's done. He could write a book about how McDonald's made their french fries. He knew they had a great potato, and he learned exactly how they blanched it. He found that out and plenty more. Don't worry, McDonald's studied Jim, too. They were so impressed with his Burger Boy operation in Columbus that studying Burger Boy became part of their training program.

M.O. #7: True operators are really curious about how things are done and want to study everything down to the last detail.

ADVISORY: If you're in the restaurant business and you find anyone matching this description, somebody who has these M.O.s, hire them tomorrow. No. Hire them today.

PART III

10

The Little Guy's Guide to Big-Time Selling

More than anything, I'm a marketer. I love to sell. I do television ads because I can reach more people on TV than I could in person. Paul Basile and Jim McKennan, who create the current Wendy's commercials, have a joke they tell. "Dave's commercials," they say, "are a lot like sausages. If you like them, you probably don't want to see them being made." Not everybody loves my ads, though, especially some slick Madison Avenue types. A reviewer for the magazine *Advertising Age,* for example, once called me "a steer in a half-sleeve shirt." He had some other unkind things to say, too, but I ignored them.

On the other hand, I have never had a very high opinion of most marketing consultants and advertising executives because most of them don't want to get their hands dirty in your business. They act like they know everything about their client's business, but they're just too lazy to get inside of things and understand them. We had one creative type who was describing our chili in radio copy. It finally dawned on me that he had never eaten our product. He never worked with us again. I think that it was stupid for the management of that agency to let something like that happen.

Our advertising people have to "do time" in the restaurants just to see what it's like. Dick Rich, who is a biggie on Madison Avenue, spent ten days touring our restaurants in 1977. When the tour was over, we asked him what he thought about Wendy's—our products and our people. "Well," he said, "what makes your food different are two things." "What are they? What are they?" I blurted out, since I couldn't hold back. "Your food is hot . . . and it's juicy." Ten days on the road for "hot and juicy," I thought to myself! But, Hot 'n' Juicy turned out to be our first national advertising campaign and one of our best as well.

In case you think I'm too hard on these folks, I'm happy to say there ARE some terrific people in the advertising profession. We've been lucky enough to work with some of the best of them, and they have really helped build our business. Our agency today is Backer, Spielvogel, Bates, and they have done a fine job for us under the leadership of Bob Lenz. They understand Wendy's, which is important. On the other hand, the reason you see so much bad advertising is that many marketing and advertising people leave a lot to be desired when it comes to learning your business.

When I first had full responsibility for a business—the Kentucky Fried Chicken places in Columbus—marketing meant "Gee, I've got to get those customers in." I would try anything. Columbus was a much bigger town than Fort Wayne, and I couldn't afford to advertise the way I did before. That meant some new tactics. I got my chicken supplier to take out a newspaper ad for me, and that doubled sales almost immediately. We did co-op ads with other local businesses. I made a deal with a guy who sold ice cream across the street from me. "Buy a half-gallon of ice cream and we'll give you a bucket of chicken." Even "Test Drive a New Car and Get a

Chicken Dinner Free!" They call these cross promotions today. Back then, they were just gimmicks to get sales up.

My accountant kept scratching his head. "If you want to make more money, raise your prices," he said. "Wrong!" I told him. "The best way to make money in this business is to make your labor costs and your rent a smaller percent of your sales. That means getting your sales up—even if you have to spend more on food costs to do it." It may not have been textbook marketing, but it worked.

The first time I met a bona fide marketing man was back at the Hobby Ranch House. He showed up one day and said, "Hi, I'm Don Hines. The Colonel just hired me to run the KFC marketing program." I asked him to explain what he did, and he told me something that I couldn't understand. Since I was real busy in the kitchen, I said to him, "Look, go check out the vegetable bins in the pantry. I think we're short of tomatoes and maybe lettuce." I gave up and just figured he was from the market. I really didn't understand what a marketing man did.

Today, I know that marketing people plan ad campaigns and other approaches to help sell products. But knowing what they do hasn't changed my opinion of them. They have plenty of charts, graphs, and research, but few have a real gut instinct for what it is that makes people want to come to a store or a restaurant. They don't understand the product they are trying to sell. That's why I believe only a very few of them.

Some marketing people think that they are creative geniuses. They forget that advertising is supposed to sell something. It's not an ego trip for the company or a chance to win some fancy award from an advertising association. Most marketing experts don't bother to think how many hamburgers you have to sell, how many sandwich makers you have to pay, or how many toilets you have to scrub to be able to afford a thirty-second ad on prime-time television (which now costs over $100,000). Some people think ads will solve everything and use them as a crutch. It doesn't work. No ad can ever substitute for a well-run business.

Our marketing department—beginning with our Executive Vice President of Marketing, Charlie Rath—is really tops because it is focused on operations. They know how much work goes into earning our advertising budget. They also know that nothing they do matters unless it supports operations and brings customers to the restaurant. We spend well over a $100 million a year on our advertising, and that's still plenty less than either Burger King or McDonald's.

Advertising is selling. When it's done on national TV, it's just done on a bigger scale, with more at risk. We were the first restaurant chain with less than a thousand restaurants to do national TV advertising. Was I scared! National advertising was big money, but I had to do it for my shareholders because they were expecting national-scale performance.

Since then I've gotten involved again from time to time, just to make sure the ads stay in touch with reality. In 1989, I got heavily involved again in Wendy's advertising. One day, I went to the agency and spent six hours explaining how we make hamburgers fresh and cook them to order. I guess I was preaching, but you could see that I believed what I was saying. That's when Charlie Rath said, "How about you being in our commercials?" I have a hard time saying my name, let alone anything else, but I told him, "I'll try, but if it doesn't work now or if it ever stops working, I'm history."

Over the years, I've learned some things about selling through advertising that works for me and for Wendy's. We get plenty of compliments on our ads, too. The CEO of Pepsi told me just a few weeks ago how much he admired what we do. Maybe a rundown of how we look at advertising will help other people in business think about how they aim their advertising.

Dave's Rules for Making a Good Ad

1. *Don't make claims for something you really can't deliver.* There are good reasons why the chief executive of many other companies isn't the spokesperson in the ad. Plenty of successful ads don't use the top manager to tell the story. His presence isn't always necessary to make the ad work. Still, no matter who is speaking for a company, an ad has to be credible. I have plenty of respect for Lee Iacocca—for what he did to restore Ellis Island and the Statue of Liberty, and what he tried to accomplish at Chrysler as its TV spokesman.

I once gave an interview about Wendy's advertising as compared to the other chains' advertising, and the reporter noticed that I couldn't bring myself to say the "M word" (McDonald's) in making the comparison. He was right. I also pointed out that ads for the other chains focused on entertainment rather than food because they can't sell the food. No one would believe them. I really think that's true.

You have to be very careful that you deliver what you claim in an ad because customers really measure your products against your claims. If you can't make a claim you can live up to, I guess you're just better off with an ad full of smiling faces.

2. *Show a sense of humor.* People say I'm funny. They say I'm good at making them smile. Well, maybe. I know I'm not real good at telling jokes or gags and delivering a great punch line. My sense of humor has more to do with smiles than with going for the big laugh. If I had to explain it, it's more that people smile when they see me in a skit and say, "Hey! I've been there."

Some of you remember an ad for the Dave's Deluxe sandwich. I'm at a cocktail party, where the waiter shoves these ridiculous hors d'oeuvres under my nose. You don't want to be rude, but you don't know what's in it, and you definitely don't want to eat it. You say to yourself: "Who comes up with these crazy ideas?" "Whatever happened to peanuts or cheese and crackers?" Or: "Why am I here? I'd rather be someplace where I would feel comfortable." We were making the point that a Dave's Deluxe sure beats a crab puff. People relate to that. It makes them smile.

3. *Don't think that a down-home, easy-going ad is either cheap or easy to make.* The actor Wayne Rogers (who used to be in the TV series "M.A.S.H.") is now host of a TV show about business for the Financial News Network called "Power Profiles." A couple weeks ago, this show did a profile on me. (I still don't know why. "Power Profiles" sounds like a series about guys like George Bush or Mikhail Gorbachev.) When Wayne said my commercials looked so easy and natural, I pointed out to him that a typical four- or five-day production for a series of television commercials costs about a million dollars. That's just to film, edit, and finish the commercials, not the cost of running them on television. A million-dollar investment can make anybody look good. The last one I made had dozens of takes and took ten hours to produce. That's for a commercial that is only thirty seconds long. So far, I've made over a hundred TV ads for Wendy's. None of them were made without a lot of effort. Not once did I ever feel that I got it all right.

You really have to be in the mood of the ad. That's not always easy. A while back, we did an ad with me driving an old Studebaker. I want to tell you, that car ad was super hard to do because I was in traffic, and I was being towed. Cars were whizzing by, and I had everybody in front of me and no TelePrompTer (a machine that fits on a television camera and shows the words you are to say). There was plenty to concentrate on. That meant I had to rely an awful lot on my director.

We try to make these ads unpretentious, but they are also extremely professional. Our people call it "shirt-sleeve sophistication." The ads aren't made for snobs, and the people we work with are the best in the business.

4. *Don't pretend to be an actor if you're not.* Whether you're making a presentation or a commercial, it's all the same. The big thing is not to be phony. I'm a member of the Screen Actors Guild, and I pay union dues. While I still haven't found the annual picnic that the union local sponsors (they have to have one, don't they?), they do have me signed up for a pension.

I may have to be a member of the actors' union, but I'm no actor. What I am is a spokesman. There's a big difference. Most business people can be convincing spokespersons if they have a product they believe in. But top guys at companies also forget that they are also lousy actors. The biggest risk that a company president or chairman faces when they do a commercial is that they will come across as having a big ego. You can always tell when the ad agency talked the boss into starring in the commercial because they wanted to flatter his ego. Everything looks staged, the boss pretends he's an actor, and everything falls flat. That's real risky for the company—because the manager isn't credible, and the commercial can't convince the audience to buy the product.

5. *Talk in a believable way.* One of our ads has me eating at a gourmet restaurant where I'm shocked at the small portion size. Everyone has had that experience. You go into a fancy restaurant and the waiter makes fun of your French. The garnish is bigger than the entree, and when they give you the bill, you wonder if you get to keep the silverware. We've all had experiences like that.

Some companies do "image advertising" that you couldn't believe in a thousand years: The employees all look like fashion-show models, the sound track sounds like it came from *Ben Hur,* and you get the feeling that the company does more good works than Mother Teresa. Remember, the words in your message can be honest and real, but if you overdo the effects and visuals, you lose being believable.

I don't even like it when we create a background that is fancier than people would expect. We had an ad not long ago for our country fried steak sandwich. The set looked like a farm J. R. Ewing would own. If Minnie Sinclair had had a farm like that back in Augusta, Michigan, I'd never have left.

6. *Make sure your customers can recognize you.* In the early days of Kentucky Fried Chicken, we had all kinds of people coming up with the way Colonel Sanders was supposed to look. In ads, on bags, and in menus, we had fat Colonels and skinny Colonels, dark-haired Colonels and fair-haired ones. We had to standardize his image into one professional look. Only then did we get the real benefits of being a brand. People know how to find you then.

7. *Be controversial.* At last count, there are 2,931 brands of products competing for attention on American television. Getting people interested enough to watch your commercial these days is very tough. Marketing people say good ads have to "bust through all the clutter." To do that, they conclude, you have to be controversial. But some of these marketing geniuses go too far. There's plenty of suggestive, risqué advertising on TV today. We think you can be controversial without forgetting about good taste. One time, an agency wanted me to say "up to your keister in biscuits," and I wouldn't do it because I felt it would offend some people.

Wendy's Kind of Controversy

Wendy's advertising has stirred up plenty of controversy, but in a quiet kind of way. We don't want to make enemies; we simply want to be noticed in the middle of all the advertising clutter that exists today, in a way that will make people remember us and have friendly feelings toward us.

I guess I'm as responsible as anyone for wanting to be a little controversial, and I've been that way for a long time. Back in the 1950s, when I was at the Hobby House, we were getting lots of compliments on our banana and coconut cream pies. We could sell even more, I thought, if we advertised. Back then, restaurant advertising on television was unheard of. But Phil Clauss was open to giving it a try. The announcer would talk about how fresh and delicious our pies were. Then, the guy on camera could feel his mouth water, and he would say he really wanted a taste. Then somebody off camera would cream the actor with a pie in the face. Sounds corny now, but it was controversial back then. Some people thought it was a mean thing to do. As far as we knew, we were the first to ever plaster people with cream pies in a TV ad. Most important of all, we sold a ton of pies and everybody in Fort Wayne talked about the Hobby House.

In May 1981 Wendy's and Dancer Fitzgerald Sample Advertising Agency of New York launched a $59 million advertising campaign: "Wendy's. Ain't No Reason to Go Anyplace Else." This campaign really grew out of a speech I had made with the theme, "Why would anyone go into a competitor's restaurant when Wendy's has the best products on the market?" It led to hefty sales increases and name recognition. I appeared in the ads, but that isn't why they were successful. They succeeded because they sounded like most people talk. Nobody ever dared to do that in a national TV ad before.

The first quarter after we ran this campaign our sales were

up 24% and earnings rose 40%. But while the registers were ringing, you could barely hear them over all the criticism. English teachers and students from all over the country wrote letters to Wendy's, telling us we were bumpkins and that we didn't know how to use the English language. "Ain't" was bad grammar. But "Ain't no"—a double negative—was unforgivable.

I got letters from twelve-year-olds saying that if they knew enough not to use *ain't,* we should, too. Another letter said, "I hope your food is better than your language." There were hundreds of articles and editorials with bruising headlines like:

BAD LANGUAGE IS NO WAY TO SELL

HAMBURGERS . . .

WENDY'S GETS A BEEF: AIN'T NO WAY

TO TALK . . .

HAMBURGER HAVEN GETS A

LANGUAGE LESSON . . .

Some groups threatened to boycott us until we cleaned up our grammar. I certainly wasn't prepared for this much controversy. Then we looked at the letters that we received—a total of only two hundred complaints. That was about one ten-thousandth of our daily customer base in the U.S. We took the press controversy more in stride, and just explained to people that we knew the grammar was wrong, but it communicated a folksy, down-home flavor that set us apart from our competition.

Slowly, public opinion began to turn in our favor. There were segments on us with Edwin Newman on the NBC *Today* show, the CBS *Evening News,* and *The Wall Street Journal.* By and large, they all agreed that even if it was poor grammar, it was great selling.

Finally, I called a press conference. I explained, "We used

the word *ain't* to attract attention. We weren't trying to tell people that ain't is right to use. We could have said, 'There is no reason to go anyplace else,' but nobody would have paid any attention to us. Did Elvis get criticized when he sang 'You Ain't Nothing But a Hound Dog'? Fats Domino had a hit with 'Ain't that a Shame.' It was all right for Helen Reddy to sing 'Ain't No Way to Treat a Lady.' So give me a break." At the end, I declared: Dave Thomas has two words for people who don't like his new campaign: Too bad!

Even though we received a lot of flak for using the word *ain't,* the campaign proved that Wendy's was a company to be reckoned with. Not only did we have the right formula, we proved we could make a deep impression on the public . . . and we had become something of an American institution.

In 1984, the so-called "Burger Wars" were in full swing. Burger King and McDonald's were slugging it out over flame-broiled versus frying. We thought that both chains were on the wrong track. We decided to change the debate. We created a new American folk hero, Clara Peller, a retired Chicago manicurist who became an overnight sensation with her now-famous catch phrase, "Where's the Beef?" She became a symbol of American spunk.

"Where's the Beef?" affected everybody. You heard or saw it on everything from bumper stickers and cartoons to Sunday sermons and songs. The "Where's the Beef?" line even got picked up in the 1984 presidential campaign, when Fritz Mondale used it in a televised debate against other contenders for the Democratic presidential nomination. I'm happy to say that the slogan worked better for us than it did for Mr. Mondale.

Josef Sedelmaier, our director, and Cliff Freeman, a senior writer at Dancer Fitzgerald Sample, created the "Where's the Beef?" slogan. They were amazed by the ad's success. They thought the lines about the "big, fluffy bun" were going to be the funny part, but it was Clara who made the whole thing work. Clara couldn't hear very well. So when it was time for her to deliver her lines, someone pinched her and she blurted out, "Where's the Beef?" just the way Joe wanted her to.

Clara was a charmer, really tuned in to life and people. She didn't want to talk about age because she said life is what you make it, no matter how young or old you are. "Age is just a number," she used to say. But we were in the middle of controversy again. Some groups thought we were making fun of older people, which was not true. Plenty more older people thought we were on their side because we showed them as spunky enough to call things like they were. Clara herself got a big laugh out of a Michigan-based group that claimed the commercials stereotyped the elderly and were demeaning to senior citizens. "If other older people can do what I do, then more power to them," she said. Before her stardom with Wendy's, Clara was just getting by on her social security. Every so often she would make $300 a day as an extra for an occasional TV ad. After Clara's commercials became a hit, her income totaled more than a half-million dollars.

Because of Clara and her sidekicks, Elizabeth Shaw and Mildred Lane, Wendy's consumer image and advertising awareness exploded. Before airing the first commercial about 37% of U.S. consumers said they either heard or had seen advertising for Wendy's. In April, following the second "Where's the Beef?" campaign, advertising awareness increased to 60%!

You have to walk the line and try to be controversial without really insulting people. It may be hard, but you have to do it. We weren't disrespectful. Mostly, we were just the first ones to get on TV and say what people were really thinking.

8. ***Don't try to please everyone.*** This may be the most important marketing lesson I know. I've sat in on plenty of marketing meetings where people tried to make everyone happy, and
it doesn't work. Go after the customers who will make a
difference to your business. Expect some people not to like
you and many more not to even notice that you exist. Spend
your time thinking about the people you really want to be
your customers. Then do everything you can to talk to those
customers in a way that will make them feel good about you.

11

Never Harass Anybody You Don't Like

The Wendy's TV ads make me seem like a nice guy, and I try to be. Most of the time. But I'm also tough on people in a quiet kind of way. If you are going to serve the customer right, that means you have to run a tight ship. Sometimes, you have to be tough on people to do that the right way.

Every now and then, I stop at the airport bookstore while I wait for a flight, and I see all these books on management. The titles are getting stranger and stranger. They're about Huns, SOBs, barbarians, and I don't know what. Maybe they have to do with management, but I never considered myself to be a Hun, an SOB, or a barbarian—so I don't know.

People are always asking me what my "philosophy" on management is. I'm not for making things too complicated, so I tell them that my philosophy of management is simply: HARASSMENT. And that's no lie.

By harassment, I mean keeping at someone until they either do what you think they should or until they change the way they act or prove their way is better. I only harass people I care about. Why should I waste my time trying to improve somebody I don't like and who probably doesn't like me, either? Harassment is a manager's biggest responsibility. If you do it right, harassment should always have a touch of fun in it. And you always have to change your tone when you're trying to tackle a real problem somebody has in doing the job, or you'll mix them up.

Dave's Rules for Successful Harassment

1. *Make sure people trust you.* I remember when Denny Lynch, our vice president of communications, first started working for us. Denny was so intense, I kept on harassing him to get him to loosen up. One day, I teased him to the brink, and he shot back, "Mr. Thomas, are you questioning my veracity?" I said, "I don't know." Then, I teased him for three more days for using a word I didn't understand. The more I saw Denny, the more uptight he looked. Finally, it dawned on me that Denny didn't trust me. He thought that since I was always on his case I was one step away from canning him. That wasn't my idea at all. Later I read something in a book called *Leaders* by Warren Bennis and Burt Nanus that stuck with me. In it, they say that Los Angeles Rams coach John Robinson "never criticizes his players until they're convinced of his unconditional confidence in their abilities." That's a good outlook to have.

As for Denny and harassment, he's totally sold on the program now. The other day, I overheard him talking to another guy I'd been badgering. "Don't worry," Denny said. "If he's harassing you, it means he likes you. If he didn't think you could take it or that you were a zero, he wouldn't say a thing."

2. *Start early.* I first met Charlie Rath, our executive vice president of marketing, in 1977. He had just "sold" Wendy's on being the local sponsor for Grand Prix Tennis—the Co-

lumbus stop on the professional tennis circuit. Every time I saw Charlie I would ask him when the signs would go up to let people know about the event. Finally, we were getting pretty close to the day the matches would start. Charlie maintained it was about three months before the tournament. I said three days. It was probably more like three weeks. Well, Charlie finally went out and did something. He had a bunch of signs screen-printed and nailed one on each of the nearly five hundred telephone poles between my house and the tennis stadium.

3. *Tell people when they're almost perfect . . . but do it nice.* When Charlie finally got the signs up, I made sure that I thanked him for the great job. Then I gave him a slip of paper with the addresses of the two phone poles he missed.

4. *Make 'em feel guilty when they do nothing.* One thing I can't stand is people who don't act on a situation. I'd rather that people make mistakes than sit around and not do something.

5. *Don't put up with excuses.* Poor results are bad enough, but weak excuses are even worse. I visit about fifty different markets each year to see Wendy's operations. When I'm on the road, I'll visit as many restaurants as I can. Most of the time, I'm happy with what we see, but sometimes not. Nothing makes me more unhappy than when I get weak excuses and alibis to explain poor performance. So, I always try to go easier on bad performance than when somebody is punting or lying.

6. *Don't let up until they go out there and find out.* Whenever our marketing people come in and tell me about somebody else's new sandwich, the first thing I'll ask is, "Did ya try it?" If somebody comes up with a new store design, I want to know what it looks like in real life. The same thing goes for

problems inside your business. You can get all the reports in the world—most of them written to cover up what the real problems are—but there is no substitute for going out there and nosing around yourself.

You've got to be real careful when you harass people. I just don't think harassment works for managers who are not perceived as nice people by their team. And if people don't know you like them and you start harassing them, they'll just clam up on you or even serve you a knuckle sandwich. But harassment can work. Why? So much of any business is detail and execution, and any manager has to stay on top of it. Harassment is personal communications. It's not some dumb, dull memo that you could just as well address "To Whom It May Concern."

7. *Batch things for people.* People tell me that I always have a bunch of lists going on in my head with messages for people. I'm a laundry list type of guy, and I've been blessed with a pretty good memory. When I see somebody, I try to go through my whole list with them. It's really just "packaging," and it's a lot better than writing a bunch of stupid memos. It's not much different from what you do with your kids as they go sailing out the door: "When did you say you were going to clean the basement? The cat's not happy with the litter box . . . and don't forget your galoshes."

8. *Make harassment fun.* Businesses focus too much on "productivity" and too little on fun. I've made more money by having fun than I have not having fun. That would be true for most people, if they gave themselves the chance. A little well-meant harassment is the best way I know to connect hard work and having fun. To me the perfect employee is someone who has fun doing the job.

I have to say that I really perfected my techniques for harassment with my children. You'll get no argument from them on that score. One year, there had been some bickering going on between the five kids, and it seemed the annual Christmas get-together was going to be a bust. I thought it was time to haul out the heavy artillery. So I called them all up and said that I had a big "surprise" for each of them that year. I didn't tell them what the surprise was, but since it was Christmastime, I think they all got the idea it would jingle in their pockets. "There's only one catch," I said. "All of you show up together for a nice Christmas lunch at the restaurant. If one of you is missing, nobody gets anything."

Molly thought that I was being controlling and manipulative. Kenny wanted to know how much time it would take. Pam said it was a goofy idea and that I would stir things up more. Wendy wanted to know why, and what my scheme was, and Lori thought it would be fun. They all showed up, and we hashed out some important things over lunch. You can call it manipulation. I prefer to think of it as constructive bribery. I reminded them they would all stick together when the chips were down, even if they squabbled once in a while. It was worth it. They gave me a card that said, "Harassment is the family form of love in the Thomas home."

Family-Style Management

I like to help make families. Through what I do to promote adoption, hopefully I've helped make a few families over the years and have made people happier for it. I also try to make families when I work. Wendy's is as much a family to me as it is a company.

Another business "family" that I've tried to help build is the team that does our commercials, and that was hard because the people involved came from all over—ad agencies, production houses, and so on.

When we first started shooting commercials, we were down in Florida, and I got the whole team together on my boat and we traveled over to a restaurant called Shooter's for dinner. Everyone was there—the makeup crew, the grips, the gaffers . . . everybody. That dinner created a personal relationship between me and everyone on the set. Their sense of pride grew because they knew I cared. Everyone from the director Billy Hudson on down through the last assistant has a personal stake in making me look good in our Wendy's commercials. If it weren't for that commitment I wouldn't want to do it . . . so I try hard not to let them down, either.

If you look at the commercials close up, you'll see many of the same people in each one. We've got our own little repertory cast: The Wendy's Theater of the Air. These people will cancel their other jobs to be there for our shoots. Our team takes pride in making great commercials. It's not "sign up, take the job, make your fee, and see you around." People don't mind coming a little early or staying a little late. Sometimes we shoot through the breaks, but it doesn't matter to the people. They say: "Let's get it done and done right."

But they also keep the tempo up and keep themselves keen. They harass one another and play jokes on each other. When we get together, it's an event. The grips—the guys who make sure everything is in the right place when it is needed—are going to have a golf tournament, and I look forward to that more than I would playing golf with most big-city mayors. When we film a commercial it's like a family reunion, a reunion that you really want to go to. That means plenty when you've gone through eighty-five takes. It would be easy for people to say to themselves, Let's just get this thing done. In every business I've been in, the key has been to get people to want to say "let's get it done right" on their own. That's why I admire my director, Billy Hudson.

Through my years in the restaurant business and in everything else I've done, I've thought plenty about how to get groups of people to work together better. I call it "family-style management," and here are some of the keys to it.

1. *Keep the family together.* The annual turnover of crew people—the number of people who leave your business each year—is very high in the quick-service restaurant industry. Wendy's was operating at a 150% annualized turnover rate about three years ago. We now have markets that are below 100%. That may sound high, but that's terrific progress. It's especially important that the basic core of ten or fifteen people stays together because they're the glue. When we studied the problem, we learned that the number one reason why we lose managers is high crew turnover; the number one reason why we lose crew members is high manager turnover. Keep the family together and you solve a lot of your problems.

2. *Give people more responsibility.* Wendy's turnover rate for restaurant general managers was 40% three years ago. This was typical for the quick-service restaurant industry. Our turnover rate today is down to 23%! What did we do differently? One thing was to INCREASE the amount of responsibility the restaurant managers had. Three years ago, a district manager—the restaurant manager's boss—had about three restaurants to look after. Now he has more than five. That means less time to look after each restaurant and more responsibility for each restaurant manager. We told the restaurant managers that they had to grow up and step into the role of being real managers. When we increased the responsibility, we also upped the rewards. We have a much stronger bonus program. In the first quarter of 1990, we paid out four times as much cash in bonuses to restaurant managers than in the quarter a year earlier. We believe in delegating responsibilities as far down as possible, but any manager who wants to dele-

gate must remember to follow through and check that the delegation gets done.

3. *Keep the home base looking good.* The number two reason why you lose crew people is because the restaurant looks like a dump. If you don't feel good enough to invest in your facility, your people won't feel excited and upbeat about working there.

4. *Help people get started.* One of the reasons that I quit my paper route was that I had no one to help me figure out how to do it. For many of the people who work at Wendy's, we are the first real job they have. Some of the crew people are disillusioned in the first couple of weeks. They didn't expect it to be like this. Management has to sit down and talk about expectations and get people through the start-up pains. It's not surprising that some of the best managers we get at Wendy's are former schoolteachers. They're just great at coaching kids. Helping people start a new job or a new duty in their job is probably the most important thing you can do to keep them confident and successful.

5. *Put your energy where it matters.* Phil Clauss and I once visited a guy by the name of Ted Cullins, who ran the Blue Bird Restaurant in a little Indiana farm community called Morristown. The building looked dull and shabby from the outside, better on the inside, and stunning in the kitchen. Ted had just put in a stainless-steel kitchen and quarry-tile floors, which were unheard of back then. He was remodeling his place from the back of the house to the front and eventually it all looked good, but he started by dealing with the basics and working out from there.

The way Ted did it sent the right message to his employees—that he was going to build the business on a rock-solid foundation, by making sure the product was right. Plenty of businesses and families would do well to learn that.

6. ***Turn challenges into contests to keep people motivated.*** Running a restaurant is a very basic business. It's also execution, but you have to keep people's interest keen. You can turn nearly every aspect of a restaurant's operation into a contest. You can run a contest for the top grillperson or the fastest sandwich maker. Our SPARKLE program is a disciplined way to keep our restaurants inspected and zeroed in on what's important to the customer. In a home, you can have kids compete for the best job of drying the dishes. In a business, it's the best job of serving the customer. The real difference is in the scale.

7. ***Don't treat people like plug-in parts.*** Grill people, cashiers, sandwich makers, and order takers all have different personalities. Our people are less interchangeable than those at most quick-service restaurants. Our jobs require a skill, and that gives people a certain role to play. Somehow, those basic skills and outlooks stick with you. When I go through a restaurant kitchen, I still think of myself as a grillman. I'm a better grillman than an order taker, for example. Jim Near is a better sandwich maker than he is a grillman. Your strongest suit sticks with you. That doesn't mean we don't crosstrain our people. Of course, you have to do that. But, you want people to feel good in their primary jobs, too—just like every one in a family has a niche, a part to play, which they can call their own.

8. ***Give people the support they need to succeed.*** I mean emotional support. Parents almost always try to give their kids the support they need to succeed. There are plenty of bosses who do not try to help their kids succeed. At Wendy's, this may mean a district manager has to support a restaurant

manager who is just starting out. Put too much pressure on a manager and you'll put him or her in a bad mood, and bad attitude spreads fast. You have to help the manager use time wisely so that the restaurant is focused on giving the most at the right time—the peak customer time. The manager's attitude will be better, and that will spread to the customer, too. He'll also organize the work better for his staff. Most of all, the manager will be there for the customers.

How do you give people support? The biggest help you can give are tips on how they might do their job easier. I knew a guy named Hep who ran a little dairy store. He would come in from time to time at the Hobby House. Once, I was busy, really busy. But he insisted that I sit down and have some coffee with him. Then he looked straight at me and said, "Dave, why don't you start running your business?" I was stunned. What did he mean by that? What did he think I was doing? Wasn't I running all over the place twelve to fourteen hours a day? That was the point, he said. If I stepped back and tried to organize the people and what had to be done a little better, I wouldn't be so frantic. That knocked me over, but there was a lot of sense to it. You have to run your business, not let it run you. A leader usually gives his people more help by letting them do their job. He can help more by standing back, sizing up the situation, and making adjustments than by taking over and trying to do everything himself.

One of the reasons that family-style management works at Wendy's is because we have a really strong human resources operation, headed up by Kathy McGinnis. In the past year, we have decentralized the company to put more authority out in the field and less of it in headquarters. We have really sharpened our training program. But maybe the biggest thing we've done is to strengthen our focus in a caring way, thinking like a family would think.

Dave's Yardstick for Measuring People

There are more than 120,000 people working in Wendy's restaurants. There are four thousand Wendy's restaurant managers alone. So we have to be pretty good at picking people. John Casey, who is our vice chairman and chief financial officer and who is a very shrewd judge of people, pointed out to me once that most of our restaurant managers are in their early twenties. With the possible exception of an infantry platoon leader in the Army, John said, he couldn't think of any other manager who is given so much responsibility so early in life. John's usually right, and I think he's especially right on this one.

The manager we pick leaves a mark on every part of the business. Nine times out of ten, you can figure out what the manager looks like from the appearance of the counter and the crew people behind it. If the crew is sharp, bright, and enthusiastic, there is a heck of a manager on duty.

1. *Know what you are picking a person to do.* When we started Wendy's some of the people we picked as franchisees were great at building businesses. They later turned out to be so-so or worse at running them. Some people are builders. Other people are operators. Today, we focus on hiring operators, and we would have been better off recognizing the difference earlier in the game.

2. *Don't make on-the-spot decisions.* One of the worst things a manager can do is to make decisions about people based simply on a gut instinct. During a dinner on one of our recent market tours, a guy came up to me and said he hocked his house for $50,000 to buy a bankrupt restaurant, turned it around, paid all the creditors off, and made $60,000. Now, he wanted to have another restaurant. Well, the story sounded

like it was made to order to appeal to me. I turned him over to the regional people. Unlike what you might expect, I don't always size people up based on gut instinct alone.

3. *Watch out for the braggarts.* There are some people you just can't stand. I'm suspicious of people who brag a lot. The quiet ones who listen well are often the best managers. The ones who interrupt you mid-sentence and who seem self-important can cause you real grief. We definitely look for team players.

4. *Check people out.* If you're considering hiring somebody, get some background from other people about how honest, how sincere, and how conscientious that person is. When they take something on, are they committed? I can always work with a person who is honest and has integrity, even if they screw up. Still, even after they're hired, I want to see what a person will do with us before I form a clear opinion.

5. *Test people's convictions.* Sometimes I will argue with people to see how well they have thought something through or how strongly they believe in what they say. A person with strong convictions doesn't have to be argumentative. Instead, they may come across as persistent or patient. Be real careful about trusting a person who changes his story on a dime just to please you.

6. *Measure people with the right yardstick.* We have some really remarkable people at Wendy's. One of them is Jerry Hamra of Little Rock, Arkansas. We just inducted Jerry into the Wendy's Hall of Fame. Jerry is a passionate, enthusiastic guy. As a kid, he had polio, but it didn't slow him down. He's been in the business sixteen years and now has twenty-two very successful restaurants. Every year, he builds two or three more restaurants. Every day, his driver takes him to the res-

taurants. He walks through them slowly and raises hell in a good-spirited way. His people love him. They know he's a leader and they trust him. If Jerry asked, they would follow him right to the top of the highest mountain.

12

Talking Dave

Whenever I walk into a Wendy's, I introduce myself: "Hi! I'm Wendy's Dad." Sometimes I'll overhear a little kid say, "Mommy, that man sounds like a television commercial."

Why I Don't Give Speeches

I'd rather talk to people than give a phony-sounding speech. I really like to talk to groups of people, because someone in the group could benefit from my message. There have been many successes in my life, and some failures. I have learned from both. A person has to share the best he has and hope that it does some good. What I think works best for an audience is to give them some good, strong, down-to-earth examples. When I give a speech, somebody will suggest an idea or an angle. Even though things get written down, nobody knows what I'll say for sure, least of all me.

The guy I really feel for is my speechwriter. He'll research it and write it and rewrite it, only to hear me tell him, "I'm not saying that." It's not that the work goes to waste. I absorb what I can, but it has to sound like it's coming from me, not off a piece of paper. Otherwise, why would people come to hear any speaker? They could just stay at home and read the same thing in a book or an article.

Whenever I give a speech, I get nervous. It doesn't matter if I'm speaking to two people or ten thousand. I used to think that was wrong, but now I know that it's just natural. When you start talking in front of a bunch of people, you never know when you might lay an egg. Over the years, though, I've learned some things about making talks, and they may help other people who have to stand in front of a microphone, too.

Talk to people, don't make speeches at them. If you spend more time picking out what dress or suit you'll wear than you do learning about your audience before you show up on the podium, you're making a speech.

If you spend more time worrying about the quotes you'll put in your talk than you do about the ideas people will take away with them after you're done, you're making a speech.

If you spend more time trying to dodge controversy than you spend trying to make a clear point, you're making a speech.

If you spend more time practicing your script like an actor than you do trying to get the key ideas down so you can talk to your audience, you're making a speech.

In my opinion, you always get the best results when you *talk* to people—one person or ten thousand people—not when you make speeches at them.

1. *Get your point across in a way that gets people's attention.* Once I opened a talk to a group of black MBA students and told them they were about to do the worst possible thing for the black community . . . and that was to be successful. My

point wasn't that their getting an MBA or being successful was bad. That was great! It was that their success would probably take them away from the communities and the people they need to help the most. They needed to be role models. That happens to all successful people. It happened to me— success took me away from the poor communities where I grew up. But if you're aware of what's happening, then you can do things to compensate for it. Well, you could have heard a pin drop after my opening comment. It really got the attention of the audience. After the talk was over, people from the audience told me that I raised a point worth hearing. So, I think the risky way I did it was worth it.

2. *Don't squeeze yourself out of your talk.* Sometimes, I bungle the language. So, I'll say "best in the bidness" for "best in the business." It's just a natural thing on my part, just like I say EYE-talian for Italian. Actually, I work hard at trying to say things right, but when you polish things so hard that you leave your personality behind, you've gone too far.

3. *Make sense to your audience.* The roughest speaking date I ever had was when I went to a small town in Ohio in 1979 to speak at a state institution for troubled youths—kids who were runaways, felons, and drug users. It was graduation day for about twenty of them, and a few of their parents came, not by choice, but rather because they had to come and pick up their kids.

The kids were worth helping, but I wasn't sure about the parents, even the ones who had bothered to come. Most were alcoholics or drug pushers. Others were just lazy and didn't want to work. These were sleaze-bags, to put it frankly, and not the kind of people I respect. How was I going to talk to them?

Until I hit my stride, I could hear a few muffled obscenities and plenty of chairs scraping around. Then I decided to keep

it simple. I stressed some ideas that the audience could remember easily. I said things like: "If you never do more than
you're paid to do, you'll never get paid for anything more
than you do."—and—"The dictionary is the only place where
success comes before work." Some of the stuff was pretty
corny, but people smiled, and some of the messages looked
like they hit home.

Whenever you're in front of a tough audience, remember,
it's the audience you have to please, not yourself.

4. *Learn what you stand for.* More people than you think
come to hear a speaker because of what that person stands for
than what the person says. After a keynote speech I gave at
one Wendy's convention, I started for the bar to get a cold
glass of grapefruit juice when I was stopped by a young,
good-looking man who had about six or seven Wendy's but-
tons pinned on both lapels of his blazer, a real Wendy's
booster. "Mr. Thomas," he said, "I just want to shake your
hand and thank you. You have been a real inspiration to me."

I didn't recognize him. "Have we met before?" I asked.
"No, sir. Tonight is the first time. But in 1976, I read an article
about you in a restaurant magazine and that article changed
my life. I was working at a Big Boy Restaurant in Kentucky
and I had lots of hopes and dreams, but I never thought I
could do anything about them because I felt I had two strikes
against me, being black and adopted. And then I picked up
this magazine in the office of our restaurant and I read about
how you were adopted and everything, but that didn't stop
you. You said that desire and hard work took you to where
you are today." This man was still holding onto my hand, so
I figured what he was saying must be pretty important to him.

"But," he went on, and you could tell he was getting a little
nervous, "I was a little, I don't want to say disappointed,
because it was a great speech, but I was a little surprised that

when you talked about how you started out and all, you didn't mention that you were adopted. Since we have that in common, I guess I was just anxious to hear more about it. You know, some details or something. But it was a great speech and all, and I'm proud to be a part of the Wendy's family."

That really registered. I used to think that people might get tired of this adoption business. You know, poor, homeless Dave and his rags-to-riches story. Now, I know that my having been adopted is an inspiration to others, and I have an obligation to get that message out.

Don't let anyone get between you and your message. In 1982, I was invited to be interviewed on a network-affiliated television station. When you do a television show, you always have to remember that the real audience is not in the studio but in front of the television sets in thousands of homes. It's like giving a talk to an audience you can't see.

The TV reporter and I were getting acquainted a few minutes before the show. Just before airtime, she said, "Now, Mr. Thomas, my plan is to talk about your competition."

I told her, "I respect that, but I want to talk about Wendy's. I want to tell you about our hot and juicy hamburgers, our new food items, and our friendly service."

With that, she pounded her fists on the table in front of us and literally screamed at me, "I do not intend to do a commercial for you!"

I remained calm and said, "O.K., fine. We'll do whatever you want to do. You ask the questions. Where would you like me to be?"

She told me to stand over there in front of the McDonald's slide. I did what I was told. The cameras started rolling.

"Mr. Thomas," she began, "you are standing next to your biggest competitor, McDonald's. How do you compete with them since they are so good and hard to beat?"

"Well," I said slowly, "I don't know a lot about McDonald's, but I do know about Wendy's." And I proceeded to give my sales pitch just like I had planned.

My point is, I was nice and polite, and I said and did exactly what I wanted. My plan was successful. The interview told the Wendy's story, and I didn't waste my time talking about McDonald's.

There were three rules I followed that made my plan successful:

- I stayed calm,
- I stayed friendly,
- and, I used her question simply to connect to my own message.

Bob Dilenschneider of Hill and Knowlton wrote *Power and Influence,* a book that offers advice on how to deal with the news media successfully, among other things. Bob's people really taught me how to focus when dealing with the media.

5. *Praise troublemakers.* Sometimes, during the question-and-answer session following a speech, I'll get somebody who raises a question just to antagonize me—not a real question, but just somebody taking a shot, like "Why doesn't Wendy's serve sushi?" or "If you guys would just study what McDonald's is doing, you'd know that a Styrofoam box is the only way to keep a burger warm." That happens to everybody who does a lot of speaking. The first thing I usually do is to praise the wiseguy and say that he is probably a lot further ahead in having thought that through than anybody else in the audience. In the meantime, I try to collect my thoughts. Then, I focus back on whatever messages I can get across that have anything remotely to do with the question. In the end, the guy is usually sorry he asked the question.

That's what I know, and I'd only add this: I'd rather be a good talker than a great public speaker any day.

Dave's Tips on Giving Criticism

The way most people look at it, criticizing is something you do naturally. "Can't you stop being so critical!?" You hear people say that every day. The way I see it, people should probably be MORE critical than they are, but most people don't know how to be critical in a way that is nice and gets results. Criticism is part of being honest. Don't be a hypocrite and tell a person who is doing a bad job that he or she is doing it right. Criticize people with the right tone of voice. That's very important.

Most companies do a terrible job of teaching their people to give criticism. No wonder that giving and taking criticism leads to so many morale problems. If you do it with the wrong attitude, people won't take it—much less so now than twenty years ago. One reason to get this right is that it's nicer to work in a company that cares about people. A second reason is that it costs an awful lot of money to keep hiring and training people to replace those who walk out on you because you're such a mean, insensitive boss. And third is that if you lose enough good people, you will get such a bad reputation, you won't be able to hire any new people at all. It all catches up with you.

At Wendy's, we spend a lot of time and effort training our people to give and take criticism. We have a super program that helps improve people's skills when they take orders over the speaker, called "Talk to Me," and we coach people on criticism a lot. We think we're pretty professional in the criticism business. So I hope you won't take it the wrong way if I give you a few suggestions on how you might improve your criticism of others.

1. *Lead the parade.* Hats are a part of the Wendy's uniform. I remember once going to three stores in a row, and nobody was wearing a hat. Not only is it a Wendy's policy to wear a hat, but it used to be a state regulation that food handlers have something on their heads to replace the old hair net. I didn't say anything at first because I am not one to walk into a store and start yelling and complaining. I don't believe in ridiculing anyone in front of others. It happened to me once and I hated it. So, I just started walking around in the stores wearing a hat myself. That started a new fashion craze and it fixed the problem.

2. *Take criticism well.* There's no better way to guarantee that the criticism you give will be listened to than to take criticism well yourself.

3. *Criticize each individual in their own special way.* Now, that's my advice, but I'm not perfect, and sometimes I just tell somebody I know, "Hey, quit being a dummy. Don't do those things." Especially if they're hard-headed . . . but only in private and only with a smile on my face.

You have to handle temperamental people differently. Criticize a sensitive person like that, and you're bound to get a sulker for a month of Sundays. With some people, you've got to sit down and talk to them, and ask them where they think they may have made a mistake.

4. *Always offer a positive suggestion.* Back at the Hobby House, Phil Clauss said this was one of my strengths. Since then, I've always made a point of giving a positive suggestion when I criticize someone. This is easy to do, and it really should be second nature for almost anybody.

5. *If nothing else works, criticize with your feet.* In 1981, I was in Detroit one afternoon for a radio interview. While I was sitting in the lobby, I overheard this disk jockey who was

going to interview me abuse one of his employees. He'd be sweetness itself introducing each song, but once the air switch was turned off, he'd lay into his assistant, calling her "sweetie" and asking where she had her brains. It wasn't just one burst of anger and he wasn't trying to make a point, he was just abusing her.

Finally, I walked into the studio and said, "Excuse me, but I couldn't help overhearing. You shouldn't treat your employees that way." I obviously ticked him off, and he shot back, "Look, you run your business, I'll run mine." So, I voted with my feet. I just left the station and wouldn't give the interview. Had I given the interview, I felt that I would just have played along with this guy's game, and I couldn't do that.

My Two Cents on Talking One-on-One

Maybe it's all this sending of messages between computers we do, all the memos that get written, or all the meetings that are called, but plenty of people in business don't know beans about one-to-one communication anymore. Here is how I handle my pet peeves.

1. *Stay focused on the other person, and they'll stay focused on you.* Make sure the other person knows you're listening. The simplest way to do that is to keep mentioning their name as you talk to them.

2. *Help other people to be taken seriously.* I'm often in meetings with a couple of other people. Jack may be talking and Harry will sit there with his eyes glazed over just being polite, but not listening to what Jack is saying. I can always tell when someone is not taking another person seriously. When that happens, I will often jump in and say, "Jack,

you've put out a really great point . . . I didn't know you were that smart." That will generally wake Harry up. Of course, I would never say it quite that way if Jack outranked me, but trying to put a funny twist on things somehow helps it go down easier.

3. *Don't use jargon.* We have three key words in our SPAR-KLE program: Quality, Service, Cleanliness. People have started to use the abbreviation Q.S.C. I hate it, really hate it. The words are *quality, service,* and *cleanliness.* When we abbreviate it, we lose the meaning of what it all means. I don't believe in abbreviation. Say the words. If you are a district manager, be a district manager, not a DM. If you're a district operations administrator, does that mean you're DOA? Don't be a DOA or an SOB or a VIP. Abbreviate things and you lose the meaning. Some people call it shorthand, but what it leads to is short thinking.

4. *Put it in a way that's natural for you.* The most important kind of one-on-one communication that happens at Wendy's is between the customer and the order taker. There are many different and acceptable ways to say, "Hey, how you doin'?" When a customer walks in. Our focus is to make sure we communicate a friendly feeling to each customer. People, even grouches, like to be treated nicely, and that begins with a proper greeting. And a proper greeting has to be heartfelt.

5. *Just get it out there.* So many managers overdo it. Instead of visiting the guy next door, they write a memo. Instead of sending out a key reminder on a card you could stick in your pocket, they do a videotape. If you want to get it across, get it out fast and say it simple.

13

Giving Something Back

I believe everyone has an obligation to put back into life more than what they take out. People who are successful have the biggest responsibility because along with the money they have the name and contacts to do the most good.

Charitable giving is not just a nice thing to do once a year. It is an investment everyone who is able should make, and it returns the greatest rewards. I have no particular plan to my giving, although I do have a soft spot for children.

I know billionaires who give away money in a very selfish way. Their "gifts" more or less support their own fancy way of life. You have to watch out how you treat people in what you do publicly. You can't afford to be domineering or arrogant: It just doesn't work. You can have all the money or all the power in the world and still not afford to be arrogant.

The charities and causes I support may not be fancy, but I am particular about why I support them. I'm proud of how these dollars are invested and think that I've learned something over the years about how to do this right. This is what I've picked up.

Dave's Charity Checklist

1. *Spread your giving around.* I think you need to help everybody a little bit, but not to stick with one thing too much. My giving has included United Way and the Heart and Kidney Foundations. Wendy has only one kidney. I also give to the Children's Home Society in Florida and St. Jude Children's Research Hospital.

I was a close friend of the late comedian Danny Thomas for a long time, and he did an incredible job for St. Jude's. Nope, he and I aren't related.

St. Jude's Hospital got some of its gifts from me in unusual ways. One day, when we had just one Wendy's, I pledged a whole day's receipts to the hospital. The day turned out to be a sales record-breaker.

On another occasion, at a PGA golf tournament in Memphis benefiting St. Jude's, both Danny and I ended up in front of the water on a par-3 hole. My partner, Charlie Rodgers, and I challenged Danny to see who could get the ball over the water and onto the green first. A hundred dollars a ball for St. Jude's was the penalty for plopping the ball into the water. Five hundred dollars apiece later, we two duffers were still at it and would probably have been hacking away into the twilight if Alabama Coach Bear Bryant, who was also a part of the foursome, hadn't joined us in the bet and finally sailed a ball over the pond.

What I loved about Danny was not just his generosity, but his down-to-earth ways. Danny was your 100% guy next door, station wagon and all. He was so real, so talented, and so committed that everyone around him wanted Danny to succeed, both as an actor and as a benefactor of St. Jude's Hospital, which is dedicated to helping children suffering from catastrophic diseases.

Some donors—especially companies—try to pump all of

their money behind one or two causes. That's not so much to help the charity as to get the donors more recognition since they lump all their giving in one or two places. They are identified with the causes they support. It works from that angle, but I think that's putting the business before the needs, and I disagree with it.

2. *Support people who make things happen.* For one gift, I chose the Dr. Arthur James Cancer Research Hospital at Ohio State University because Dr. James is a Horatio Alger recipient and a man of fierce dedication. If there's a cure for cancer, Dr. James and the people at that Center will find it. I'm hoping my gift to the Center will make it the best in the nation, with a reputation like Sloan Kettering in New York and M.D. Anderson in Houston. I was really gratified when Wendy's executives and our suppliers matched my gift.

The Children's Home Society of Florida has five thousand volunteers, and it's another priority for me. The volunteers in that program are as likely to be drill press operators as chairmen of the board. In fact, one family—a truck driver and his wife—took in more than twenty kids in a single year. People in his neighborhood actually helped him build an addition to his house. Every year, we honor these people at a banquet and present the R. David Thomas Child Advocate Award. Last year Burt Reynolds and Loni Anderson came, and they also contributed generously.

3. *Give to charities that really put the bucks to work.* Some people are leery of giving to charities because there's been a lot of talk about how funds are misspent. I don't believe in charities where the money is skimmed off so that organizers drive around in Cadillacs and BMWs and wear expensive suits and dresses courtesy of the contributors. Donors should speak up when something doesn't look or feel right. We have a right to ask questions and hold people accountable.

4. *Don't let yourself be manhandled by a charity.* Most charities are grateful for the help you give. But not all of them. Not long ago, I received a recognition award from a charity. It started out as a routine testimonial where they charged $100 a head to a fund-raising dinner, and that was fine, but then they leaned on me to set up private cocktail parties to raise even more money. It didn't stop there. They called up friends and business associates and asked them to sponsor deals. Before long, instead of an honoree, I felt like a sales tool. To top it off, on the night of the dinner, right before my acceptance speech, a lady walked up to me and asked how much more money could they sign me up for. That did it. I was fried. I said, "I'm going up there to receive this award, and I'm really shocked that you would ask me that now."

When I got to the podium, I felt like telling the audience exactly how this outfit did business, but I didn't. What I did instead was a lot smarter, I think. First, I started my talk by saying that this event was honoring a really good cause, but that there were plenty of other good causes, too, and people should spread their money around. I talked about Recreation Unlimited and the Ohio State University Cancer Hospital and a bunch of other charities. I had the microphone and did I use it! As you could guess, there were plenty of shocked, sad faces when I glanced up at the professional fund-raisers sitting on the dais.

5. *Look for ways to support education.* Education gives a person the opportunity for a better life, and every person is entitled to that. That's why I support schools, universities, and educational organizations like Junior Achievement. Each year, we support scholarships for 4-H and the Future Farmers of America students. Since we're in the food business, smart farming is pretty important to our future.

In 1987, I made a substantial dollar contribution to Duke

University in Durham, North Carolina. That donation built the R. David Thomas Center for executive education, part of the Fuqua School of Business. My neighbor in Florida, the entrepreneur and industrialist J. B. Fuqua, is as sold on the importance of education as anyone I've ever met. J.B. also believes in results. So when he asked me to build a Center adjoining the Fuqua School, I knew the investment would make a difference for generations to come.

The Center gives executive education for managers who aren't studying for a degree like an MBA. But I could never keep those guys at Duke happy. Not only did they give me those chairs I told you about because they couldn't find a seat in my restaurants, they made up a "Where's-the-Beef?"-style song called "Where's the Grits?" because they couldn't find any Southern cooking on a Wendy's menu.

6. *Give first priority to local causes.* Not only will you be able to see the impact, you have the best chance of having a voice in the way the dollars are used. Recreation Unlimited, a camp for the disabled in Columbus, Ohio, is one of my favorite causes because it helps people help themselves. I was asked to get involved by a local TV sportscaster, Jimmy Crum, and a business friend of mine, Larry Liebert. Seeing this camp develop and grow has been a highlight of my life. On my second visit there, I was greeted with a sign that brought a smile to my face. It read, WELCOME, OUR DAVID THOMAS. Jimmy had introduced me to everybody on my first visit and they mistook the *R.* David for *Our* David.

Sometimes I'll get together a busload of people to go out and see the camp. Once folks experience it, it's very hard to turn away. When people see what's being done, once they see that you have a human connection—that you know the staff and other people there on a first-name basis—it's like being invited into another family.

Another local charity I support is the Charity Newsies. Every year around Christmastime, hundreds of former newspaper boys sell papers on Columbus street corners. They raise over $200,000 and every cent is used to buy new clothing for kids. I'm an honorary member since I didn't have a paper route for long. Another project I've been behind is Buckeye Boys Ranch—a residential treatment center about fifteen miles from Columbus that cares for teen boys with emotional problems and learning disabilities. There's nothing else like it in the world.

When I first blew on the scene in Columbus and started to get involved in local projects, I'm sure some people looked at me as some nouveau-riche dude who got lucky and hit it big. But cramming down seven-course dinners with the country-club set never meant too much to me. When I had the money to invest in the community, I was determined it would go places that would do some good.

In addition to what I do personally, Wendy's and its franchisees are really active in the community, in national organizations like Kiwanis, Lion's Club, and the Rotary. When I walked into Wendy's headquarters on a Monday morning last month, I saw our results on the United Way campaign. We had hit 120% of our goal, and the campaign wasn't even over. Not many companies can boast of an attitude toward giving like that.

When special needs come up, we try to get involved, too. When the Persian Gulf crisis broke out, we worked with a Columbus television station, a radio station, and a car dealership to collect items like sunscreen, razors, and insect repellent for our troops over in Saudi Arabia. Our restaurants were drop-off points, and we collected over 500,000 pounds of needed items. They tell me it's the largest airlift of gifts to U.S. troops during a wartime effort. It's a real grass-roots, Midwestern attitude, I guess, but our people love it . . . and it makes a difference.

That Family Feeling in Government

Another way you can give something back is through taking an interest in government and the issues that are important to the public.

For example, we've been a step ahead of the competition for a long time when it comes to nutrition. Today at Wendy's you'll find a brochure on nutritional facts that has more, clearer details than you'll find on most grocery-store packages. I'm proud of the fact that Wendy's has been out ahead of most of the quick-service restaurant industry on the issue of waste. Because we use paper wrappings for our sandwiches and very little Styrofoam, the public has seen us in a different light than some of our competitors. Every little step helps. We have reduced the package weights for our pickle containers, mustard, and mayonnaise . . . and they're cheaper than the old containers were, too! Waste stirs me up. Our country cannot afford waste.

The list of issues is endless, and the issues aren't confined to the U.S. alone. We won't buy South American beef at all. Much of it has grazed on former rain-forest land, and we're concerned about the ozone layer and the environment like everybody else. It's impossible to run a big company, and probably not even a small one, without keeping tabs on issues like these, and that means a lot of contact with people in government. My kids are even more involved than I am. My daughter Pam now runs the volunteer program for the city of Columbus, coordinating the work of six thousand citizen volunteers.

I have met a lot of politicians and there are some I can't

stand. They are too impressed with themselves and forget about the people who worked hard to put them where they are. Former President Gerald Ford isn't like that. He is a very warm, nice, and caring man. I met him when he was still in office at a golf game at Burning Tree, with Defense Secretary Melvin Laird, and Ohio Governor Jim Rhodes. I'll never forget that President Ford nearly hit the governor's security man, Vern Metz, with a golf ball, and I very nearly did the same with the President!

What astonished me about Gerald Ford was his ability to focus on what he was doing. Although the world's issues were clearly there on his mind, he was still able to remember the names of Governor Rhodes' security people after only meeting them once. He offered them food and drinks and treated everyone like family.

President Ford invited us back to the White House for dinner. When we arrived at 1600 Pennsylvania Avenue, he showed us around, since it was our first visit. When we entered his personal quarters there was a lady outside the door to their bedroom waving her arms and telling us to stop. Mrs. Ford was getting dressed. The President wasn't going to let that stop us, but I said, "Mr. President, maybe we should wait until Mrs. Ford is finished." He laughed and said, "O.K., we'll give her a few minutes." He yelled through the door, "Betty, I've got some friends out here and we want you to join us for dinner." It was just like going to dinner at neighbors down the block.

We ate in the residence dining room, which was surprisingly plain. We were served a meat-and-potatoes meal, and it was the experience of a lifetime. After dinner, the President asked if we wanted to stay all night since there was a heavy-duty storm going on outside. "Come on now, Dave," President Ford said with a smile, "isn't the Lincoln Room good enough for you?" "No, no," I said, "we really have to leave." The truth was I was embarrassed that I didn't have my shaving kit. Talk about somebody worrying over the wrong things! When I think about that chance I missed to stay in President Lincoln's room, I'll never forget how thoughtful President Ford was . . . or what a dumb decision I made when I declined.

President Bush is like President Ford in many ways. He's a basic, honest man, and he's really strong on family values. That's why I was especially proud when President Bush asked me to help promote the "Adoption Works . . . for Everyone" program.

Why Adoption Is My Thing

As I explained on the *CBS This Morning* Show to Harry Smith, President Bush has challenged me to encourage adoption, especially the adoption of the more than thirty thousand special-needs children who need permanent homes—youngsters who are older, who are members of minority groups, who are emotionally or physically disabled, or who are part of sibling groups.

So far, I've been in touch with the heads of America's one thousand largest companies, the Fortune 1000, urging them to offer adoption benefits to their employees. Wendy's has this program now, and President Bush has called it a model for the nation. Eligible employees can receive both financial aid and paid leave to help support an adoption. The company pays up to $4,000 for adoption-related expenses and up to $6,000 toward the adoption of a special-needs child. There's a paid leave, similar to maternity leave, after the adoption takes place.

When I was thirteen, I learned that I was adopted and born in Atlantic City, New Jersey. My mother had been in a home for unwed mothers. When Grandma Minnie told me that I was adopted, I felt my stomach turn, and I was really afraid. Then I was angry that no one had told me sooner. She sensed my frustration and resentment and really went out of her way to make me feel good about myself.

My mother's name was Mollie, and I first learned more details about my birth family from Minnie Sinclair when I was twenty-one and had just gotten out of the Army. I learned from Grandma Minnie that my mother Mollie had lived around Philadelphia, so I went there to try to find her. For some reason I went to the police station's missing-persons department because I didn't know where to start. An officer looked at my adoption papers and Mollie's letters to Minnie and found an address in nearby Camden, New Jersey.

I went to the address in Camden and met my grandfather, who was a tailor, and my grandmother, who was then very ill. I can still remember the sewing machines and different-colored spools of thread. They told me that my mother had died from rheumatic fever, just like my adoptive mother, about two years before. I learned that Mollie had worked in a restaurant for a while as a waitress. She married a man named Joe and never had any other children.

They didn't tell me anything about my birth father. I don't know if they really didn't know or just wouldn't tell me. But I felt it was a deep, dark secret. However, having reached half my goal, I decided not to press them further. I just accepted the fact that I might never know who my birth father was.

Years later when my children were raising their own families, they started asking me again about my birth father. They were looking for family medical history for the various school applications they needed for their kids. My daughter Pam decided to investigate. From my birth certificate we learned that my dad's name was Sam. She started calling people in the Philadelphia area until she found the wife of one of Sam's cousins.

Pam arranged a trip and our family went to meet Sam's relatives. We learned that he was single until the age of thirty-five, had worked as a stock broker, and had a son who is now a college professor. Sam had passed away years before Pam's call. When I met his family, they said that they'd never heard of my mother and didn't think that my dad even knew I was conceived.

It may sound strange to you that I should support adoption, because my adopted childhood was not all that happy. That's not the way I look at it. Adoption made it possible for me to get Minnie Sinclair's love and teaching. Adoption gave me my adoptive mother's care and affection in my early years, even if I don't remember it. And although he had different values than I grew up to believe in, my adoptive father tried his best. Had I not been adopted, I could have ended up as a ward of the state or raised in a county orphanage. So the way I see it, adoption turned out to be a big plus for me.

So, now you know all my secrets.

There are five reasons why adoption means enough to me to make it my personal crusade. Let me tell you those reasons:

1. There are kids who are growing up living in makeshift orphanages made out of converted office space and worse in some parts of this country. That shouldn't happen in the most powerful country in the world.

2. Without a home and affection, the chances for making it in this world are mighty slim.

3. Children raised out of homes often end up in trouble and as burdens to society. Go check out the welfare roles and the prison rosters if you think I'm wrong.

4. If you have had the blessing of a good home life yourself, then you do owe something back.

5. The world works on families, it really does. Don't let fear stop you from being an adoptive parent. I wrote this recently for *Guideposts* magazine, and I really believe it: "When you do the thing you fear the most, God might well have a pleasant surprise for you."

14

Checking Your Spark Plugs

A couple of weeks ago, a photographer took my picture for some company report. Before we started, I said to him, "No double chin, okay?" He took me seriously and kept telling me to keep my chin up. He kept saying, "Keep your chin up. Keep your chin up." "Brother," I said to myself, "you don't know how these packages are put together." What used to be normal posture for an eighteen-year-old grillman is close to an Olympic warmup for somebody going on sixty. Things change. So I want to leave you with a little of my philosophy of living and the way I look at things today. The best place to start is with my heroes, the heroes who have stood the test of time.

Everybody has their own cast of heroes when they're growing up. I used to go to the movies as a kid, and Roy Rogers and Gene Autry were my first heroes. Everybody has a need for heroes, I think, people to mold themselves after, people they want to be like. You have to be able to dream, but those dreams should be about real people who have actually done things. When I look back, there were nine people more than any others whom I have really looked up to and who helped me become the person I am today. They're my All-Star Team, my Hall of Fame. Some of them are still role models today, because people need role models—I think—at every stage of their life . . . not just when they're kids.

Dave's Hall of Fame

Minnie Sinclair:

Most Memorable Trait: Her gumption. I remember her working in her garden *and* holding a part-time job at a restaurant, and how well she managed while raising four children on her own.

Most Vivid Memory: When she told me I was adopted. Instead of letting me feel alone and rejected, she helped me feel special and wanted.

Most Important Lesson: She always said, "Don't cut corners, or you'll lose quality. If you lose quality, you lose everything else."

The Regas Brothers

Most Memorable Trait: Their drive. Frank Regas came over from Greece on a steamer and worked himself up from being a $20-a-month dishwasher to co-own a restaurant with his brother George.

Most Vivid Memory: Frank Regas hustling around his Knoxville restaurant in a three-piece suit, bussing tables, and doing whatever else it took to stay on top of things.

Most Important Lesson: Try—really try—and you can do anything you want to do.

Phil Clauss

Most Memorable Trait: His openness. An openness that helped him spot the opportunity Kentucky Fried Chicken represented, encouraged me to be creative, and allowed him to give me an opportunity to buy part ownership in the Columbus restaurants, which later made me a millionaire.

Most Vivid Memory: How Phil turned around the attitude of the staff one afternoon when he challenged us to be constantly on the move.

Most Important Lesson: Let each day teach you something. Go out and look for new ideas.

Colonel Harland Sanders

Most Memorable Trait: His total and absolute commitment to his product. No matter who owned the company, it was always "The Colonel's chicken."

Most Vivid Memory: The day I met him, when I was just assistant restaurant manager. He spent time with me and treated me just like an equal.

Most Important Lesson: Keep your standards high because the customer has high standards.

Kenny King

Most Memorable Trait: His values. He loved the good things in life, but he never let them own him.

Most Vivid Memory: The $15-dollar tip he gave a waiter after a dinner in the Cleveland Athletic Club back in the early fifties, and his belief that he had the obligation to give back something from what he earned.

Most Important Lesson: Hey, son, this is America. If I can do it, so can you. All you have to do is work hard and have ethics.

Len Immke

Most Memorable Trait: His encouragement. His patience and moral support helped me found Wendy's.

Most Vivid Memory: Sitting in the steam room of the Columbus Athletic Club as the last part of the plan for Wendy's clicked into place.

Most Important Lesson: The best way to help people make up their mind is with a little coaching.

Norman Vincent Peale

Most Memorable Trait: His energy. How he has always let his enthusiasm for what must be done give him the energy to stay active and positive.

Most Vivid Memory: His presenting me with the Horatio Alger Award—the same award once won by Kenny King and Harland Sanders.

Most Important Lesson: That problems become solutions when people look at them with a positive attitude.

George Bush

Most Memorable Trait: His persistence. The President's ability to persevere in the Persian Gulf crisis where human rights and personal freedoms were at risk. He has given Americans a renewed sense of pride and patriotism, and revitalized our country's stature around the world. I predict he will be remembered as one of the greatest presidents in history.

Most Vivid Memory: Being asked by the President to be spokesman for his special initiative on adoption.

Most Important Lesson: Leadership means the ability to set priorities and to stick with your goals, even when the going gets rocky.

Surviving Success

I was thirty-seven when I felt I'd really made it. What I've learned over the past twenty years is how to live with success . . . and that's hard. People usually don't worry about that. "Just let me succeed," people pray. They think they'll deal with the problems success may bring later. The truth is, those problems can come up overnight. You'd better be prepared for them.

I remember the great successes Wendy's had in 1984. We launched one of our most successful new products ever, the hot-stuffed baked potato. And Clara Peller spoke out for us in the most memorable campaign in the history of advertising. All of this created one great big positive jolt for us, but it also created two problems: the problem of the "ermine robes" and the problem of the "silver bullet."

First, ermine robes. Royalty is nice, but I know there is no royalty in business. If you think you are king of the hill one day, someone is sure to knock you off the next. You will lose your focus on the business if you worry about how important you are. That happened at Wendy's. Pretty soon you start tripping on your own ermine robes because you believe you can't make a mistake. Your ego starts to make decisions—not your brain. In our case, we tripped up on our breakfast menu before we regained our footing and our sense of perspective.

Next, silver bullets. A great success like the "Where's the Beef?" advertising campaign can lead you down a dead-end road. You're not as tough-minded about what you need to do to solve problems because you believe another silver bullet will come along and bail you out. Wrong! We let the success of "Where's the Beef?" cause us to lose focus on operations and disciplines. Silver bullets are boomerang bullets. One day, they're soaring away from you. The next day they're whistling back, ready to smack you in the forehead.

1. *Don't just study people who succeed, study people who handle success well.* See how people who have succeeded financially live their lives, and learn from that. Some people can't handle money or success. It destroys them. They overbuy, drink, take drugs, become playboys or country-clubbers. Eventually they let their businesses slide, too, because they let their egos get in the way of their judgment. They forget about their families, their self-respect, and their fellow human beings.

2. *Know when to let go.* It was back in the early eighties that I turned over most of the day-to-day management of Wendy's to other people. All the administration, the committees, and the paper-shuffling weren't my thing. Instead, I decided that I would do what I do best: visit with people in the stores, preach about my standards, look for new product ideas, and good-naturedly harass people.

I was lucky to be able to do it because we had Bob Barney on board, along with Ron Fay—recruited from W. T. Grant's food operation (clearly the best thing Grant's had going for it). The two of them set up the transition to Jim Near today.

It was great the way Colonel Sanders hung on to Kentucky Fried Chicken as "his" product, wanting to uphold the highest quality standards and all. But it was sad that the Colonel couldn't let go of the day-to-day business, even when he really had nothing to do with it anymore. I vowed I would never be like that. Instead, what I wanted was a "slow-motion" hand-off of Wendy's to the management of the future, and it makes me proud to know that's what we have had.

3. *Get a sounding board.* For years Kenny King was my friend and sounding board. We would talk on the phone for two to three hours and I would ask his opinion on different deals I was considering. I would ask, "Is my thinking right on this, Kenny?" He would give me his opinion, or mention something that I hadn't thought about, or tell me that I was screwing up. I didn't always agree with him, but I always had respect for him. And he built up my confidence. I have never quite found someone to replace Kenny King. Today, several people act as my sounding boards. Len Immke is still one of the best. It's even more important to have good, honest sounding boards AFTER you're successful or after you've become a top manager. After all, who wants to take the risk of telling you the truth when you're the boss?

4. *Look at what your success will let you do next.* Find something new. I've been experimenting with car dealerships and golf courses and doing more with charities and good causes. Because I have these other interests, I'm able to make the best contribution to Wendy's because I don't have the urge to be back tampering with the everyday business.

What Makes You Go?

Many people have asked how I kept myself motivated, especially when times were tough. When I was growing up, I didn't have a mother or father to encourage me. There was no one person pushing me, although there were many who helped me and influenced my thoughts. I guess I just had a burning desire to make something of myself. In the beginning it was a matter of survival. Then it became something I just couldn't shake off even after I'd been a financial success.

Back in the chapter on how Wendy's started, I had some tips for people who might want to open their own business. I think you should also take a look at "What makes you click"—put the focus totally on you first and not even think about a business you might open.

There are ten questions you can ask yourself to help figure out if you really should take the risks that go along with being your own person and building your own business. Think of this list as your personal inventory as you do a quick scan of these questions. Then read on and see if the discussion of these ten questions can help you to fine-tune your answers.

Here are the ten questions:

1. After I achieve something, do I like to go ahead and do something new?

2. Am I willing to commit all my time and energy to an idea?

3. Do I have self-confidence?

4. Do I like to work with people?

5. Am I willing to slice the pie?

6. Do I want to be an innovator or a creator?

7. Even when things are going good, am I always trying to fix problems?

8. Am I always trying to learn from others?

9. Do I think there's a solution to every problem?

10. Can I rely on my business intuition?

1. *After I achieve something, do I like to go ahead and do something new?* Do you like to sit back and savor it, or is the success quickly yesterday's news as far as you're concerned? I'm not saying that sitting back is wrong. I often wish that I could, but achieving the last challenge doesn't stick with me long. It's never enough. When I got the food business going in the Enlisted Men's Club or turned around the Columbus Kentucky Fried Chicken operation, I wanted to move on to do new things. Most entrepreneurs are like this.

2. *Am I willing to commit all my time and energy to an idea?* I've already mentioned how much time and work is needed to start a business. You'd better know if you're prepared to be singleminded about something. The best way to find out is to look at your past. Have you done it before? Did you like doing it?

3. *Do I have self-confidence?* I firmly believe a person can do anything he or she wants to do. I also believe a person can *NOT* do something if they don't want to. It's a matter of personal choice. It helps if you have self-confidence, if you believe in yourself, and have family and friends who believe in you, too.

Once you have self-confidence, that doesn't mean you have it for life. Everybody gets screwed up now and then. My self-confidence gets shaky from time to time, especially when I look at certain people and think they are smarter than me. Self-confidence is something most of us have to work at constantly. We have to think positive thoughts, and take care not to let the jerks of this world get us down. Some of the most unlikely people will try to shake your confidence by throwing their education, their money, or their social position in your face. They try to make themselves feel big by making you feel small.

4. *Do I like to work with people?* There is nothing I ever achieved that didn't involve plenty of other people. You can't do it alone, that's for sure. And, remember: Who's going to run the business and keep it going if you decide you want to move on and do something else?

5. *Am I willing to slice the pie?* Along with liking to work with other people, you have to be able to share the successes— to give others an ownership stake and part of the rewards. People who are focused on themselves and don't enjoy sharing usually don't make good entrepreneurs.

6. *Do I want to be an innovator or a creator?* At Wendy's, we're innovators, but I don't know how creative we've been. In my mind, the difference between being innovative and being creative is that creators invent things, innovators use inventions in new ways. We've done a lot of innovative things: The Pick-Up Window and the square hamburger are two. We didn't invent the salad bar or the stuffed baked potato, but we were the first ones to put them into a national chain of quick-service restaurants.

Creators like to perfect things, innovators want to apply them. Entrepreneurs in business are mostly innovators, I think.

7. *Even when things are going good, am I always trying to fix problems?* Back in 1975, when the Wendy's business had been opened only six years, I used to keep a list of all the stores in the bottom 10% of sales. Whenever a store hit that group, we would throw in extra promotion, more advertising, and coupons. It was a simple program, but it worked, and it saved a lot of stores that proved later to be winners from being closed in the early days. Some people like to polish the best of what they do better; I'm more concerned with getting everything up to the same high standard.

8. *Am I always trying to learn from others?* Keep thinking, "How can I improve myself and do better?" One way is to learn from other people and not resent them for their success. I never resented anyone for owning anything. I just wanted to figure out how I could own something myself. Too many people spend all of their energy being resentful and jealous, instead of using that energy to benefit themselves. The bottom line is to find out how someone became successful, learn from that, and then go out and do it.

9. *Do I think there's a solution to every problem?* No problem is too small because small problems can grow into big ones. For example, every now and then, I get claustrophobic. It makes me nervous to ride in elevators and in the backseat of cars. One time I was riding in the backseat of a limousine with President Gerald Ford and I started feeling closed in. Instead of going into a panic and spoiling the day for myself, I looked out the window and stared outside. When I am on an elevator that is crowded, I get off at the next floor and wait for one that is not so full. But I don't stop riding elevators. Just don't ever stop looking for solutions.

10. *Can I rely on my business intuition?* Can I live with the downside—really live with it? Can my family live with it, and do they understand it as well as they should? Lots of people will bravely say, "Let's go for it. It doesn't matter if we're broke tomorrow." But they don't try to imagine what they would have to sacrifice if they only had half of their current income and none of their benefits for a few months.

On the other hand, if you need lots of studies and information to make decisions, it's risky to be on your own in business. You can't afford either all the time or the money to get that kind of comfort. Had I said, "Let's go research this Wendy's idea and see how we make a niche for ourselves," the first Wendy's would never have been built.

Tom Lester, who is both one heck of an automotive engineer and a close friend of mine, grew up—he says—when "innovation was a necessity." He started a small manufacturing business in an old horse-blanket factory and, out of it, built the premier aluminum die-casting firm in America. He later sold it to ITT.

When Tom first got Ford as a customer to buy his regulator body assemblies for cars, Ford was experiencing a rejection rate of 40% for this part. He pledged to reduce the rate to 5%, and in fact, got it down well below that. Tom sums up his guiding principle in one phrase: "Good enough is not good." Tom's business intuition was so sound that he caught on to the growing need for quality long before it became the number one battle cry in American industry.

Before you go risk everything on your intuition, you better ask yourself if you have a good gut feel. Have you been able to predict trends? Have you looked at different businesses and been able to call which ones would work and which ones wouldn't and why? If you're going to go by instinct, you better have good instincts.

If your answer to most of these question is yes, then you may have the kind of personality to be an entrepreneur, at least as far as my life as an entrepreneur has taught me.

In a way, my achievements were made easier by having such a rootless life in my early years. Had I grown up on a street in a small town with a set of family and friends, there would have been the temptation to sit back, relax, and enjoy life. As it was, there was nothing to hold me back from looking for more.

How I Stay Happy . . . and Dissatisfied

Because I always have kept moving, my life today is both happy and dissatisfied. I wouldn't have it any other way, and here's what I do to keep my life fun and on an even footing.

Everybody has toys—things we buy to give us pleasure—and they're O.K. within reason. But you have to make sure you own the toys, and not vice versa. I have spent my share of money because I like to buy things, especially toys like boats and cars, but there was always enough in the bank to cover them. If I make a profit on something, I sometimes reward myself by buying a new toy. My first gift to myself was a diamond ring. I don't know why I bought it because I don't really like jewelry. I was probably just trying to imitate the Colonel and Kenny King. Both had rings like that. My second big purchase was a Cadillac Fleetwood. Since then I've owned almost every kind of new automobile. I don't collect them or anything; I just drive them for a while and then trade for something new and different, whatever is "hot" at the time. Some people who are well off talk about their "collections." They sit around admiring them, polishing them, and guarding them. I could never understand that. Do they own the collections, or is it the other way around?

My biggest, most expensive, and probably most stupid purchase was a ninety-one-foot, custom-built yacht that carried a multi-million dollar price tag. Buying it was bad enough, but to maintain the thing and keep it running with a crew of four cost me tons of money! As I explained to a reporter from *The Saturday Evening Post* a few years ago, I wanted to have a boat from the day my adoptive father took me on a motorboat ride over Gull Lake near Augusta, Michigan, when I was just a kid.

One year after buying it, the sheer stupidity of the expense got the better of me. It wasn't that I couldn't afford it. It was why I needed to. So I sold the yacht to a business associate of mine. In a short time, he realized that he was just paying for misery, too. I'm glad I had the experience of owning a yacht, but reckless spending is not in my blood. The way I see it, it's O.K. to like nice things, but not if they own you.

1. *I know my own insecurities.* Especially the fear of losing what you have. Off and on for years I've found myself laying awake nights worrying about being poor again. I think about it a lot because I remember the days I didn't have anything or anyone. I don't know if I can ever relax and say, "I have so much I can stop worrying now." But at least this fear has never turned me into a reckless spender or a miser. My fear of being poor has never caused me to hoard my money or be selfish with it, either. It has never kept me from giving to others. I like to give to people, to charities, to education, and to the less fortunate.

2. *I try to stay encouraged.* Your fears and self-doubts are your personal traps. You may say, "I've never done it before, how do I know I can do it?" Well, you don't know. There are never any guarantees, but there are also no rewards without risk. Talk positively to yourself because your own negative thoughts will hold you back more than another person will. Talk to friends who sincerely care about you and use their encouragement to keep you going.

3. *If I get depressed, I just do something different for a while.* When Phil Clauss offered me four bankrupt KFC stores, although I knew it was an opportunity, deep down I was afraid, and there were times when I got depressed. When that happened, instead of defeating myself, I made an effort to change my thoughts. I forced myself to believe that I could do it, and then went back to working hard and giving it 150%. Kenny King told me, "If you make a mistake, don't let it

block you. Go do something different." Putter in the garden. Do something for your church. Take your kids bowling. The trick is never to let yourself wallow in being unhappy.

4. *I tried never to saddle my kids with my own ambitions.* Some people say, "I'm not going to give my kids a free lunch. I'll make them work for everything they get, just like I did." Spoiling my kids is not one of my major problems in life. They are my kids, and if they are spoiled by my giving and can't handle it, that's their problem.

I never had any career expectations for my kids. I didn't need a doctor or lawyer in the family. I just wanted them to be honest and try to live good, decent lives. I thought it would be nice if they went to college, but if they didn't want to, that was their business. I was always more interested that they brought home the right attitude rather than an "A" report card. Looking back, however, I should have been tougher on their education and encouraged all of them harder to get their college degrees.

I always wanted a relationship with my children, but since I wasn't around much, it didn't develop until they got older. By then it was their choice. As they got older they decided to have a relationship with me. I like to think that I didn't change; *they* changed because they got to know me better. The real truth is that I have changed, too. Maybe I have more time now and am more willing to see their point of view. (I'm not sure it was so smart to put that admission in the book. I can already see one of my kids opening up the book and pointing to it next time we have a "debate.") Lorraine really raised the kids, and I guess I was sort of a stranger to them for a long time. I'm not proud of that; it's just the way it was.

The main thing I want to pass on to my grandchildren is that they can go out and be anything they want to be. But I'm going to push education a little harder with my grandchildren.

A good education gives a person more self-confidence. I've always had to fight for everything, and I think that with an education you don't have to fight quite so hard. You have more choices open to you, and you can choose without as much fear of failure.

5. *I try to help other people.* A newspaper reporter asked me at my home in Florida how I'd want to be remembered one hundred years from now. I told him that's not one of my major concerns in life. I'm not sure I want to be remembered. I mean, if I'm dead, why would I care about it, anyway? I'd rather be remembered while I'm living.

For now, my television career is helping in that department. One lady was nice enough to write and tell me that the only two TV personalities she wanted to meet were me and Billy Graham!

There isn't anything in my life that I haven't been able to do. Well, maybe there is one thing. I would like to be able to sing like Perry Como or Nat King Cole. Throughout this book, I have preached that a person can do anything he or she wants to do. Maybe someday I'll wake up and decide to take singing lessons. It sounds like something I'd do . . . and imagine the commercials they could cast me in then!

Author's Note on Adoption Works

As I tour the country telling people about adoption, many folks get interested. They ask me a lot of tough, detailed questions about just how the adoption process works. They are all good questions that don't necessarily have simple answers.

So I asked some well-known adoption groups to help everybody out by compiling information on how to get the adoption process rolling—or just to learn more about how adoption works.

The guide on the following pages is the work of these experts. I'm real proud of it, because I think it dispels some of the myths and misunderstandings about adoption.

I was adopted and I feel strongly that adoption could help many children today. To all those people considering adoption I want to say "thank you." Believe me, it means a lot to know that you're thinking about giving the gift of a loving family to a child who desperately needs it.

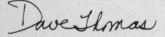

Adoption Works . . . For Everyone
A Beginner's Guide to Adoption

Every Child Deserves a Family

If there is one thing all children deserve, it's a loving family. They deserve the love, attention and guidance of a nurturing mother and father.

But it doesn't always work that way. Thousands of children of all ages, throughout this country, don't have a permanent family—and they're looking for help.

One way you can help is by considering adoption.

Adoption is a big step. Naturally, hundreds of questions spring to mind:

- How do you adopt a child?
- What's the difference between private and public agencies?
- Who is eligible to adopt?
- What does it cost?
- Where do I go?
- What type of children need to be adopted?

Adopting can be a long and sometimes bumpy journey. But the rewards can be truly wonderful. The bottom line is: The more questions you ask, the better off you'll be. The simple goal of this guide is to get you started on your way.

Why It's Important to Ask Questions

The process of adoption is not governed by a single set of national laws and guidelines.

Be prepared to be flexible when you begin the adoption process. Adoption laws vary from state to state. Adoption groups and agencies may have different policies and guidelines as well.

So as you read on, understand that the process of adoption can be a little confusing—and that's why it's so important to ask questions and get as much detailed information as possible.

Why People Adopt Children

People who adopt children want to know the joy of helping a child grow up to be a happy and fulfilled adult. They may be people who cannot have a child or they may have had children and "have room for one or two more" in their homes and their hearts. Adoptive families share a strong desire to provide love and care for a child. The most important ingredients for adoptive parents in the relationship are maturity, love and acceptance.

Children Needing Adoptive Parents

There are all kinds of wonderful children waiting to be adopted—babies, toddlers, older children, even teenagers! Here are a few examples:

- One family adopted two sisters, ages 14 and 16. "Almost grown" and living in a group home, they still wanted parents. They wanted someone to provide guidance and emotional support. When these girls are adults, they'll want to call or be home just to chat and exchange greetings on Thanksgiving and other holidays. And perhaps someday, they'll bring home a beloved grandchild to visit. The parents, in their late forties, adopted the girls because their children were grown up and they still had plenty of love to give. Adoption was a happy solution for everyone involved.

- Valerie was 10 when she was adopted. Her adoptive family, the Thompsons, had a teenage son and daughter and they all

wanted more children. Valerie had been abandoned by her
mother and had lived with five different foster families since
being placed in foster care at age 6. She wanted a permanent
family.

She visited the Thompsons several times before the social
worker gave the placement approval. In the spring, she became a family member.

Because Valerie was so proud of her new family, she hoped
to assume the family's last name before school started. And
just a few weeks before school, the judge finalized Valerie's
adoption and she was now an "official" Thompson. The
whole family celebrated afterwards.

- Infants also need adoptive families. Some infants are placed
  for adoption by parents who are unable to raise a child.
  These parents want their child to know the love of a carefully
  chosen family who is eager to parent a child.

  For example, Jimmy's mother tried to parent her baby but
  by the time Jimmy was two months old, she realized she just
  couldn't handle the demands of parenthood. She chose
  adoption for Jimmy. The Anderson family was thrilled when
  they received a telephone call from their adoption agency,
  telling them about little Jimmy. The soon-to-be Mom and
  Dad cheered, danced around the living room and jumped up
  and down because they were so happy!

- Some children are placed for adoption by state social workers because the children have been neglected or abused. It is
  rare that a child needs a family because the child's parents
  have died, leaving the child an orphan.

  Timmy and Susie, ages 6 and 8, had been abused and
  neglected by their parents and were in foster care for several
  years when the Randalls adopted them. A year after the
  adoption, with the assistance of continuing therapy and the
  compassion and understanding of their parents, they are
  adjusting well. The school has identified Susie's learning disability and created a good plan for her. Timmy is hyperactive
  and is receiving medication and treatment from the family's
  physician. The children have made a lot of progress and a
  good future lies ahead for them both.

What Is Adoption?

Adoption is the permanent, legal transfer of all parental rights from one person or couple to another person or couple. Adoptive parents have the same rights and responsibilities as parents whose children are born to them. *Adoptive parents are real parents.*

There are two common kinds of adoption. One involves relatives—usually stepparents—adopting the child or children of the person they are married to. The other involves adopting a child or children who are unrelated to the adopting parents. It is this second kind—the "unrelated adoption"—that this guide examines.

Getting Started: The Home Study

Before children are adopted, they may live with foster parents or in a group home or other institution. Sometimes, newborn babies are placed with the adopting parents directly from the hospital and sometimes they are placed with the adoption agency's foster families for several days or weeks.

In most cases, a home study (sometimes called an adoption study) is required to adopt a child. Usually, social workers working for licensed adoption agencies perform the home study after a family has applied to an agency and a preliminary screening process has occurred.

A home study is not just a visit to the home of people who want to adopt to see if it is clean and neat. Much more information is gathered to make sure the people hoping to adopt are ready for parenthood and also to help them understand how to become good parents. And importantly, adoptive parents don't have to be "perfect" or "rich."

Prospective adoptive parents are asked many questions. For example: Why did they decide to adopt a child? What type of child would they like to adopt (an infant, a school-age child, more than one child, and so forth)? If a married couple wishes to adopt, they will be asked how long they've been married and if they both want to adopt. Many times one person is more eager to adopt than the other, but it's important to make sure both of them truly want to adopt a child.

If the person applying to adopt is single, she or he will be asked many of the same questions as a married couple. They will also be asked if other family members might be available to help with the child. For example, the parents, brother or sister of a single person might be willing to babysit and agree to be available if the parent becomes sick.

There are no magic answers to the questions a social worker asks to help a family determine if they are ready for adoption. Instead, the worker will take everything into account, including whether the prospective parents have any experience with children, either by working with children in their jobs, helping care for relatives' children or in some other way.

The social worker will make sure the adopting family can afford to parent a child. In most cases, the adopting parents must get a complete physical examination to make sure they are healthy enough to become parents.

The social worker also will examine more practical considerations. Where will the child sleep? Is the home safe? Will it be "child-proofed?" Will one of the parents stay at home to care for the child or will the child attend day-care? These questions will help prospective parents consider other important issues.

The home study or adoption study is also an educational experience and an opportunity for prospective parents to learn about important adoption issues, such as how and when to explain adoption to a child. If the family plans to adopt an older child or children, they will learn about behavior that may be displayed by children who have been abused or neglected, and receive suggestions on effective parenting.

The home study process is also a chance for families to assess their own strengths and approaches to parenting.

Many agencies offer group classes which provide education to families considering adoption and an open forum to discuss prospective parents' questions. In some cases, families make long-term friends with other people in their class who plan to adopt children.

Adopting an Infant

People who have read and heard about the much publicized "baby shortage" may believe it is virtually impossible to adopt an infant. It's true there are many people interested in adopting infants, but that doesn't mean it's impossible. If you would like to adopt a baby, contact good, ethical adoption agencies in your area or identify reputable attorneys, and read as much about adoption as you can. Another helpful way to learn about adoption is to find other people who have adopted.

Contact your state adoption specialist or other reliable groups experienced in adoption to check out agencies, attorneys and other sources.

You can use the time while you wait for your child to prepare yourself for parenthood by reading about adoption and talking to adoptive parents. Many hospitals and colleges also offer low-cost adoption classes which could be helpful. In addition, one task you can do during your waiting time is to identify a good pediatrician for your child.

Adopting a Child With "Special Needs"

- Carlotta, 15, a reserved Hispanic girl, is an outstanding student who receives weekly counseling to deal with past problems of abuse and neglect.
- Tamika, 8, and Travis, 11, are African American siblings who have a strong bond and have always depended on each other. They have emotional problems which they are learning to cope with.
- Jerry, 9, is a white child with mild cerebral palsy and borderline mental retardation. He likes school and is an affectionate child.

These four children are among thousands with special needs who are in foster care, group homes or other institutions and are waiting for adoptive families. Some children with special needs are infants in the custody of private adoption agencies.

The term "special needs" refers to many categories of children, including those with physical or emotional disabilities, healthy school-age children, and children with brothers and/or sisters who need to be adopted.

In addition, there are African American, Hispanic and children in other ethnic groups who need families. Although most adoption groups do not believe ethnicity alone should result in a child being considered to have a special need, federal and state regulations consider ethnicity within that category.

The fact is children of all races and ethnic groups, as well as multi-ethnic children, need adoptive families. There is room for every child to be adopted and room for nearly every family to be qualified to adopt, regardless of race or religion.

Special Challenges for Children With Special Needs

"Special needs" is a phrase that replaced "hard to place" in describing many of the children who need to be adopted.

Many children with special needs are physically or emotionally disabled due to circumstances inflicted upon them by others and they need someone to help them turn their lives around.

But imagine the thrill of putting a smile on the face of a lonely and scared child who has never known love! Or the joy of seeing a child, your child, succeed at an achievement no one thought was possible: running a mile, reading a book, actively participating in a club.

The important thing to remember is that the words "special needs" cover many different situations. The common denominator is the urgent need for a family.

A child with special needs may be retarded or may have a high I.Q. For example, theoretically a twelve-year-old athletic genius is considered a child with "special needs" if she needs an adoptive family. Why? Because of her age. And if she had a brother, she would have another "special need" because she'd be a member of a "sibling group!"

In the case of children with medical disabilities, the disability may be curable. For example, a child may be born with a cleft palate which can be surgically repaired. One family adopted a baby girl born with a hernia and had it surgically corrected.

However, many other medical or emotional disabilities are not as easily corrected.

Siblings also need families. Whenever possible, siblings should be kept together. One family adopted three sisters and one brother after seeing them on a local television news program called *Wednesday's Child.* Through the TV program, the prospective parents learned of classes for people interested in adoption. The couple took the classes and adopted the children. Today, the entire family is active, participating in Scouting together.

Many state social services offices, as well as other organizations, have listings or photographs and descriptions of children who need families.

Some qualities that are important to parents who adopt children with special needs are: Flexibility, patience, good problem-solving skills and a willingness to identify local community resources.

Many Foster Children Need Adoptive Parents

Why do children enter and sometimes remain in foster care? When children are removed from their families because of abuse, neglect or abandonment, state or county social workers try to help the family resolve their problems. But in some cases, despite everyone's efforts, these children must leave their home.

While social workers are trying to both assist the family and protect the children, the children may live with a foster family or in a group home.

A foster family differs from an adoptive family in that it is temporary. (Although in many cases, children remain in foster care for years, often with many different families, and their only chance at a permanent family is through adoption.)

A foster family knows the child may be returned to the family of birth or to relatives, or may be placed for adoption. Foster families usually receive some financial and medical assistance for their foster children.

After a period of time that may last several months to several years, and when the problems of the child's original family cannot be resolved, the agency which has custody of the child may go to court to legally terminate parental rights. The reason is children need to have a permanent home. Social workers will then try to find a good adoptive family for the children. In about half the cases, the foster parents become the adoptive family.

Some children in the custody of the state have medical problems when they are adopted. For this reason, Medicaid, a state and federal program of medical assistance, may be continued. This means that the child may be eligible for free medical care. Medicaid is not offered for all children with special needs, but may be available for your child, even after the adoption is legally finalized.

For example, one family adopted a child with fetal alcohol syndrome. He is a loving and wonderful five-year-old who has some serious physical problems because his mother drank alcohol excessively before and during her pregnancy. Because of this problem, his adoptive parents receive Medicaid benefits for him.

Sometimes a "subsidy" is available to adoptive parents when the child needs special care. This means parents will receive a monthly payment from the state until the child reaches age 18. (In some states, subsidies continue until age 21.)

If you are interested in adopting a child with special needs, contact local adoption agencies for more information. You'll be invited to meet and talk about adoption or application forms will be sent to you. The process should be explained thoroughly. If you have any questions, ask them! Don't be afraid to ask.

Using Agencies to Adopt

About two-thirds of all adoptions are arranged by private or public adoption agencies. There is a difference between "public" and "private" adoption agencies. A public agency is a state or county agency which places children and is supported by your tax dollars. The private agency is in most cases licensed by the state, but operates using fees from adoptive families and/or charitable contributions. Most private agencies are nonprofit organizations.

Private adoption agencies may have a religious sponsorship. Some agencies specialize in finding families for infants while others see their mission as placing children with special needs. Many agencies place children with and without special needs.

Adoption agencies screen adoptive parents and provide counseling to them. Some provide classes on adoption and teach prospective parents about the various issues involved in understanding adoption; for example, how and when to tell your child about adoption. Some agencies assist families with questions or issues which arise after the adoption is legally finalized.

Agencies also help pregnant women or others who are considering placing their children for adoption. Agencies even counsel the children themselves, if they are old enough at the time of the adoption or later on, when the children or adopted adults may have questions.

Although the majority of adoption agencies, attorneys or others involved in the adoption process are honest and helpful, there are a few which have questionable practices. Agencies or attorneys may charge high fees or retainers in full when the person applies, without provisions for refunds of any kind.

Be sure to review the standard procedures of any agency you plan to use.

Check out the adoption agency by contacting your State Adoption Specialist, an individual at your state Social Services headquarters, usually in the capital city. Find out from your local state social services office the phone number of the state office, or contact several of the resource organizations listed at the end of this chapter.

Ask the State Adoption Specialist if the agency you plan to work with is licensed and in good standing. Also ask if there have been any complaints or investigations about the agency. Consider calling adoptive parent groups in your area and ask them if any members have had experience with this agency.

If possible, get names of people who have adopted children through this agency. Names may be available from the agency or from parent groups. Call the adoptive parents and ask them if it's convenient to discuss their agency experience with you.

Adopting a Child from Another Country

Thousands of children who live overseas in foreign orphanages need families. About 9,500 children from other countries were adopted by U.S. citizens in 1991, part of a trend that is likely to continue. International adoptions are rapidly changing and so are the rules.

U.S. citizens can adopt children from Asia, Latin America, Eastern Europe and other countries. Currently, most of the adopted children come from Korea and other Asian countries.

International adoptions are complicated to arrange. It's important to work with someone, whether it's an agency, group or individual, who is ethical and experienced.

If you would like to adopt a child from another country, you must have a home study of your family. This is a requirement of the U.S. Immigration and Naturalization Service (INS). In most cases, the adoption agency or person who is helping you will also assist you in finding a child who needs a family.

Independent Adoption

Private or public adoption agencies are one resource through which a family may adopt a child. In most states, you may also adopt a child by using the services of an adoption attorney or other intermediary. An adoption which is not arranged by an adoption agency is called an "independent adoption."

Some people choose independent adoption because they believe that an adoption agency would not accept them. They may be over age 40, not married for very long or have another situation that they think might cause them to be rejected by an agency.

Others seek the services of an attorney because the agencies may have a waiting list of several years.

In some states the attorney or intermediary will identify a pregnant woman considering adoption, just like an agency might, while in other states it is up to the adopting parents to locate the woman.

Sometimes parents adopt a child born in another state. In this case, the family must comply with the laws of both states. Both attorneys and adoption agencies place children out of state, although attorneys probably arrange more out of state placements than do adoption agencies.

It is important to find an ethical and competent intermediary, one who will follow all the laws and treat everyone involved fairly.

Laws vary greatly from state to state. Your lawyer should be familiar with what is and isn't allowed in the state. For example, in some states, it is lawful to pay the medical expenses of a pregnant woman planning an adoption. In other states, it is illegal to pay for such expenses. In some states, it is legal to pay the reasonable living expenses of a pregnant woman (rent, clothes, etc.). In other states it is illegal to pay such expenses. *In all states, it is illegal to buy a baby.*

Directly giving money or gifts to a pregnant woman who is considering adoption (or to the father of the baby or other relatives) could be construed as baby buying. In some states, baby buying is a felony, which could lead to a jail sentence. To make sure there are no legal problems, it is best to allow the attorney or intermediary to give any support payments to the pregnant woman or mother.

To find a good and ethical adoption attorney or intermediary, ask local parent groups if any of their members have successfully adopted children independently.

Talk to adoptive parents who have used the services of an attorney or intermediary. Remember to respect the privacy of adoptive parents, in the event that they don't wish to talk or answer questions.

Questions to Ask an Agency or Attorney

When you have located an agency or attorney and you are thinking about applying to adopt, you will want to know the following: Does the organization concentrate on placing infants or older children? (Most attorneys place only infants.) What type of adoptive parents do they seek?

Ask an adoption agency how long will it take from applying to the agency to the start of the home study.

About how many children did they place last year? What preparation classes, seminars or readings do they require of adoptive parents? What supervision will occur after the child is placed with your family but before finalization of the adoption? (Most adoptions are finalized by the court about six months after the child is placed.) What assistance can the agency provide after the adoption?

Who May Adopt

State laws vary when it comes to answering the question of who may adopt. However, there are a few guidelines. For people seeking to adopt infants, most agencies are looking for parents who are under age 40, married at least three years, financially secure and healthy. This does not mean that people over age 40 or single adults can never adopt a baby.

Many agencies have increased their upper-age limit to over 40. In some cases, the age of the husband and wife is averaged. And some agencies have eliminated age limits.

If the agency places children with special needs, then the 40-year age limit is usually waived. Social workers will take into account the individual family situation.

Many people who plan to adopt infants don't have children and some agencies prefer childless couples or couples who have only one child. If the family wishing to adopt has two or more children then they should seek an agency which does not have this rule or an independent adoption.

Sometimes the agency or attorney considers whether or not the prospective parents are infertile; other times it is not considered relevant.

Many people think an adoption agency under religious sponsorship is likely to give preference to adoptive parents of their faith group. However, that is not necessarily true. It's always best to ask.

Fees to Adopt

Adoption fees vary from state to state and depend on whether the family is adopting an infant or an older child. Whether the family uses a private or public agency, an attorney or intermediary also affects adoption fees.

In general, infant adoption fees are the highest, because the agency or attorney often must include prenatal care costs including childbirth delivery. As a result, fees to adopt an infant can range from nothing to around $30,000.

Fees over $20,000 should be examined carefully. The average fee collected for adopting healthy infants by one group of agencies belonging to the National Council For Adoption (NCFA) was $9,200, according to a 1992 survey.

When a family adopts an infant with special needs, agencies sometimes waive or lower their fees.

If the child is placed by a public state or county adoption agency, financed by tax dollars, fees will be minimal or there may be no fee at all.

It is extremely important to obtain fee information in writing from any agency, attorney, intermediary or consultant before starting the home study process. This way you will be sure you can afford the agency or attorney's fees. You should also have a written explanation detailing the fees, what they cover and what "extras" you may be responsible for later.

Adoption Benefits

Increasing numbers of forward-thinking corporations now offer adoption benefits as part of their employment benefit package. Corporations such as Apple Computer, Inc., Coca-Cola, Gannett Company, IBM, Time Warner, Walt Disney Co., Wendy's International, and others provide their employees with time off for adoption, financial assistance to adopt and other benefits designed to promote adoption.

In addition, many health insurance plans cover the adopted child from the time of placement in the home, and in some cases the newly adopted infant is covered from birth. As of this writing, in Arkansas, Florida, Georgia and Kansas, for those families with family health insurance prior to the infant's birth, insurance companies are required to cover adopted infants.

These laws are designed to give adoptive parents and children the same insurance protection as parents have when children are born to them.

Be sure to check for any exclusions in your benefits policy relating to pre-existing conditions. (Note: Many large corporations have self-insured medical programs which may not be subject to state law.)

Military members on active duty also may now receive reimbursement for up to $2,000 of adoption fees through licensed agencies.

Adoptive Parent Groups

There are hundreds of adoptive parent groups nationwide and many are very helpful. A helpful adoptive parent group can provide a hopeful parent with a chance to meet other people who feel good about adoption and who have adopted children. It's also a chance to meet adopted children and see them interact with their parents.

Good adoptive parent groups often provide the most realistic information on parenting adopted children. They can tell you of the joys and the heartaches. They can wisely encourage you and at times discourage you—either way, you gain a fuller understanding of the reality of adoption.

In addition to the emotional support, many adoptive parent groups can offer a wealth of information for hopeful parents. Often they will know which agencies and attorneys are the most ethical and helpful and they can usually suggest other resources in the community.

To locate the adoptive parent group closest to you, contact one of the national groups listed at the end of this chapter.

Talking About Adoption Positively

When talking about adoption, unfortunately many people use outdated language. Positive adoption language refers to adoption in a favorable, sensitive and nonjudgmental way. For example, the phrases "give away" or "put up for adoption" are negative. Most adoption experts prefer "place for adoption" or "made an adoption plan."

Think about it: If a woman makes the difficult decision for adoption, is it fair to say that she is "giving away" her child? Also, the phrase is inaccurate. Children cannot be given away because there is always involvement of the state in an adoption; for example, adoptions are legally "finalized" by a judge in a court of law.

A "real" parent is a parent by birth or by adoption. Some adoption professionals prefer the word "birthmother" for the woman who gives birth to a child who is then adopted. Most people involved in adoption do not like the phrase "natural parent," an old legal term, because it suggests to some that adoptive parents are "unnatural."

"Unwed mother" is viewed by many experts as a negative term. A better phrase, if marital status is relevant, is "single mother."

If the parents' marital status is relevant, then "born to unmarried parents" is a better phrase than the word "illegitimate."

The phrases "adopted person," "adopted woman," "adopted man," "adopted child" are all preferable to "adoptee." Take care when describing someone's adoptive status. For example, it is inappropriate to refer to someone's four children as three children and their "adopted son," setting that child aside. Only if specific references are being made to when the child was adopted or other relevant issues are being discussed should the child be identified as an adopted person.

It is better to say a person "was adopted" than "is adopted." Adoption is not an ongoing legal process. The adoption occurred at a certain point in time in the past. If need be, another good term is "He is an adopted person."

When Adopted Kids Grow Up

There are about 5 million people living in the U.S. today from all walks of life who were adopted. Some of them have grown up to become famous achievers: Olympic Gold Medalist Scott Hamilton . . . Dr. Wilson Riles, a noted California educator . . . Dave Thomas, founder of Wendy's Old Fashioned Hamburgers restaurants . . . NBC-TV celebrity Faith Daniels . . . and President Gerald Ford . . . all were adopted.

This doesn't mean the children you adopt will become famous celebrities when they grow up or that you have to be famous yourself to adopt. More than anything, children who are adopted need the caring of a good family and loving, accepting parents. And maybe you could be that parent to a child who waits for you.

Conclusion

Though we have covered a lot of ground in this guide, we can never hope to answer all of your questions about adoption. If you are interested in learning more about adoption, contact one or more of the organizations listed at the end of the guide. Your letter or phone call may be the first step leading you to adopting a child.

Glossary of Commonly Used Adoption Terms

Adoption—The legal transfer of all parental rights and obligations from one person or couple to another person or couple.

Adoptive parents—An individual or couple who have chosen to adopt and have received court approval.

Foster parent—An individual or couple who has temporary care of a child but has no legal rights in determining many aspects of a child's life. Sometimes foster parents become adoptive parents.

Home or adoption study—The social investigation, study and preparation of a family who wishes to adopt. Usually this includes a visit to the home and talks with family members. It includes background checks to verify employment and good character.

Special needs—Refers to many categories of children, including children with physical, emotional or medical disabilities, healthy school-age children, children with brothers and/or sisters who need to be adopted and minority children.

Stepparents—Sometimes confused with adoptive parents. A stepparent is the spouse of a child's parent. A stepparent may become an adoptive parent by legally adopting a child.

Termination of parental rights—This can be through a voluntary process, wherein the parent(s) the child is born to consent to an adoption. The termination of parental rights may also be against their will, if the state feels doing so is in the best interests of the child. A termination of parental rights must occur before an adoption can be finalized. Sometimes foster children are placed with families when it is expected that the parental rights will be terminated. After the termination occurs, then the children may be adopted.

Waiting children—Another term for children with special needs, especially children who need families.

Waiting period—The period after a family is approved for adoption by an agency until a child is placed with their family.

Resource List

AASK America/Adopt a Special Kid
657 Mission St., Suite 601
San Francisco, CA 94105
(415) 543-2275

Adoptive Families of America (AFA)
3333 Highway 100 North
Minneapolis, MN 55422
(612) 535-4829

American Academy of Adoption Attorneys
Box 33053
Washington, DC 20033-0053

Children Awaiting Parents (CAP)
700 Exchange St.
Rochester, NY 14608
(716) 232-5110

The Institute for Black Parenting
9920 Lacienega Blvd., Suite 806
Inglewood, CA 90301
(310) 348-1400

National Adoption Center (NAC)
1218 Chestnut St.
Philadelphia, PA 19107
(215) 925-0200

National Council For Adoption (NCFA)
1930 Seventeenth St. NW
Washington, DC 20009
(202) 328-1200

North American Council on Adoptable Children (NACAC)
1821 University Ave., Suite. N-498
St. Paul, MN 55104
(612) 644-3036

U.S. Department of Health and Human Services (HHS)
200 Independence Ave. SW
Washington, DC 20201
(202) 619-0257